P9-DGU-519

Daniel C. Mack
Editor

Collection Development Policies: New Directions for Changing Collections

Collection Development Policies: New Directions for Changing Collections has been co-published simultaneously as *The Acquisition Librarian*, Volume 15, Number 30 2003.

Pre-publication
REVIEWS,
COMMENTARIES,
EVALUATIONS . . .

"**W**ELL WRITTEN AND TIMELY. . . . VALUABLE for organizations coping with outdated collection development policies or where policies are non-existent. . . . Covers many issues related to librarians and collection development practices and policies."

Peter Linberger, MLS
Business Librarian
The University of Akron

WITHDRAWN

More pre-publication
REVIEWS, COMMENTARIES, EVALUATIONS . . .

"TIMELY AND COMPREHENSIVE .... Offers insight on a range of topics from digital collections and electronic resources to remote storage and local cataloging practices. THE ISSUES RAISED AND SOLUTIONS OFFERED ARE INVALUABLE to those responsible for collection development policy as well as those affected by it. Using case studies from Penn State University, Berkeley, Simmons College, and St. John's University, the book addresses the history of collection development and policy statements, subject-specific policy statements, and the publicizing of policy statements."

Margaret W. Hughes, MLIS
*Humanities, Social Sciences &
Africana Cataloger
Stanford University*

"A USEFUL SNAPSHOT of how changing times not only inform answers to questions of policy making, but reformulate the links between collection development staff and technical services, systems, and instructional staff. . . . Provides a compendium of frontline 'practices and projects' reports documenting mostly ARL libraries' recent responses to the organizational, space, budgetary, and publishing issues that the writers and users of such policies face."

Robert H. Kieft, PhD, MLIS
*Librarian of the College
Haverford College*

"Includes examples of documents currently in use in academic libraries and policies created for specialized areas of the collection. The analysis of subject-specific statements and of policies of RLG libraries based on ALA criteria made available on the Internet is particularly helpful for academic libraries with specialized collections."

E. A. Glasgow, MLS
*Reference Librarian
Newton Falls Public Library*

Collection Development Policies: New Directions for Changing Collections

Collection Development Policies: New Directions for Changing Collections has been co-published simultaneously as *The Acquisitions Librarian,* Number 30 2003.

The Acquisitions Librarian Monographic "Separates"

Below is a list of "separates," which in serials librarianship means a special issue simultaneously published as a special journal issue or double-issue *and* as a "separate" hardbound monograph. (This is a format which we also call a "DocuSerial.")

"Separates" are published because specialized libraries or professionals may wish to purchase a specific thematic issue by itself in a format which can be separately cataloged and shelved, as opposed to purchasing the journal on an on-going basis. Faculty members may also more easily consider a "separate" for classroom adoption.

"Separates" are carefully classified separately with the major book jobbers so that the journal tie-in can be noted on new book order slips to avoid duplicate purchasing.

You may wish to visit Haworth's Website at . . .

http://www.HaworthPress.com

. . . to search our online catalog for complete tables of contents of these separates and related publications.

You may also call 1-800-HAWORTH (outside US/Canada: 607-722-5857), or Fax 1-800-895-0582 (outside US/Canada: 607-771-0012), or e-mail at:

docdelivery@haworthpress.com

Collection Development Policies: New Directions for Changing Collections, edited by Daniel C. Mack (No. 30, 2003). *An in-depth guide to building and maintaining effective policy statements.*

Acquisition in Different and Special Subject Areas, edited by Abulfazal M. Fazle Kabir (No. 29, 2003). *Presents profiles, methods, and processes for acquisitions in specialized subject areas, including local and regional poetry, oceanography, educational information in electronic formats, popular fiction collections, regional and ethnic materials, and more.*

Strategic Marketing in Library and Information Science, edited by Irene Owens (No. 28, 2002). *"A useful overview of marketing for LIS practitioners in a number of settings, including archives, public libraries, and LIS schools." (Barbara B. Moran, PhD, Professor, School of Information and Library Science, University of North Carolina-Chapel Hill)*

Out-of-Print and Special Collection Materials: Acquisition and Purchasing Options, edited by Judith Overmier (No. 27, 2002). *"Offers inspiration and advice to everyone who works with a special collection. Other librarians and bibliophiles who read it will come away with a new appreciation of the challenges and achievements of special collections librarians. . . . Also valuable for teachers who address these aspects of library work." (Peter Barker, PhD, Professor of the History of Science, University of Oklahoma, Norman)*

Publishing and the Law: Current Legal Issues, edited by A. Bruce Strauch (No. 26, 2001). Publishing and the Law: Current Legal Issues *provides lawyers and librarians with insight into the main areas of legal change that are having an impact on the scholarly publishing world today. This book explores constitutional issues, such as the Communications Decency Act, showing how the First Amendment makes it virtually impossible to regulate the World Wide Web. This unique book includes a history of copyright law up through current international treaties to provide an understanding of how copyright law and the electronic environment intertwine.*

Readers, Reading and Librarians, edited by Bill Katz (No. 25, 2001). *Reaffirms the enthusiasm of books and readers as libraries evolve from reading centers to information centers where librarians are now also web masters, information scientists, and media experts.*

Acquiring Online Management Reports, edited by William E. Jarvis (No. 24, 2000). *This fact-filled guide explores a broad variety of issues involving acquisitions and online management reports to keep libraries and library managers current with changing technology and, ultimately, offer patrons more information. This book provides you with discussions and suggestions on several topics, including working with vendors, developing cost-effective collection development methods to suit your library, assessing collection growth, and choosing the best electronic resources to help meet your goals.* Acquiring Online Management Reports *offers you an array of proven ideas, options, and examples that will enable your library to keep up with client demands and simplify the process of collecting, maintaining, and interpreting online reports.*

The Internet and Acquisitions: Sources and Resources for Development, edited by Mary E. Timmons (No. 23, 2000). *"For those trying to determine how the Internet could be of use to their particular library in the area of acquisitions, or for those who have already decided they should be moving in that direction . . . this volume is a good place to begin." (James Mitchell, MLS, Library Director, Bainbridge-Guilford Central School, Bainbridge, NY)*

Gifts and Exchanges: Problems, Frustrations, . . . and Triumphs, edited by Catherine Denning (No. 22, 1999). *"A complete compendium embracing all aspects of the matter in articles that are uniformly well-written by people experienced in this field." (Jonathan S. Tryon, CAL, JD, Professor, Graduate School of Library and Information Studies, University of Rhode Island)*

Periodical Acquisitions and the Internet, edited by Nancy Slight-Gibney (No. 21, 1999). *Sheds light on the emerging trends in selection, acquisition, and access to electronic journals.*

Public Library Collection Development in the Information Age, edited by Annabel K. Stephens (No. 20, 1998). *"A first-rate collection of articles . . . This is an engaging and helpful work for anyone involved in developing public library collections." (Lyn Hopper, MLn, Director, Chestatee Regional Library, Dahlonega, GA)*

Fiction Acquisition/Fiction Management: Education and Training, edited by Georgine N. Olson (No. 19, 1998). *"It is about time that attention is given to the collection in public libraries . . . it is about time that public librarians be encouraged to treat recreational reading with the same respect that is paid to informational reading . . . Thank you to Georgine Olson for putting this volume together." (Regan Robinson, MLS, Editor and Publisher, Librarian Collection Letter)*

Acquisitions and Collection Development in the Humanities, edited by Irene Owens (No. 17/18, 1997). *"Can easily become a personal reference tool." (William D. Cunningham, PhD, Retired faculty, College of Library and Information Service, University of Maryland, College Park)*

Approval Plans: Issues and Innovations, edited by John H. Sandy (No. 16, 1996). *"This book is valuable for several reasons, the primary one being that librarians in one-person libraries need to know how approval plans work before they can try one for their particular library . . . An important addition to the professional literature." (The One-Person Library)*

Current Legal Issues in Publishing, edited by A. Bruce Strauch (No. 15, 1996). *"Provides valuable access to a great deal of information about the current state of copyright thinking." (Library Association Record)*

New Automation Technology for Acquisitions and Collection Development, edited by Rosann Bazirjian (No. 13/14, 1995). *"Rosann Bazirjian has gathered together 13 current practitioners who explore technology and automation in acquisitions and collection development . . . Contains something for everyone." (Library Acquisitions: Practice and Theory)*

Management and Organization of the Acquisitions Department, edited by Twyla Racz and Rosina Tammany (No. 12, 1994). *"Brings together topics and librarians from across the country to discuss some basic challenges and changes facing our profession today." (Library Acquisitions: Practice and Theory)*

A. V. in Public and School Libraries: Selection and Policy Issues, edited by Margaret J. Hughes and Bill Katz (No. 11, 1994). *"Many points of view are brought forward for those who are creating new policy or procedural documents . . . Provide[s] firsthand experience as well as considerable background knowledge. . . ." (Australian Library Review)*

Multicultural Acquisitions, edited by Karen Parrish and Bill Katz (No. 9/10, 1993). *"A stimulating overview of the U.S. multicultural librarianship scene." (The Library Assn. Reviews)*

Popular Culture and Acquisitions, edited by Allen Ellis (No. 8, 1993). *"A provocative penetrating set of chapters on the tricky topic of popular culture acquisitions . . . A valuable guidebook." (Journal of Popular Culture)*

Collection Assessment: A Look at the RLG Conspectus©, edited by Richard J. Wood and Katina Strauch (No. 7, 1992). *"A well-organized, thorough book . . . Provides the most realistic representations of what the Conspectus is and what its limitations are . . . Will take an important place in Conspectus literature." (Library Acquisitions: Practice & Theory)*

Evaluating Acquisitions and Collections Management, edited by Pamela S. Cenzer and Cynthia I. Gozzi (No. 6, 1991). *"With the current emphasis on evaluation and return on funding, the material is timely indeed!"* (*Library Acquisitions: Practice & Theory*)

Vendors and Library Acquisitions, edited by Bill Katz (No. 5, 1991). *"Should be required reading for all new acquisitions librarians and all library science students who plan a career in technical services. As a whole it is a very valuable resource."* (*Library Acquisitions: Practice & Theory*)

Operational Costs in Acquisitions, edited by James R. Coffey (No. 4, 1991). *"For anyone interested in embarking on a cost study of the acquisitions process this book will be worthwhile reading."* (*Library Acquisitions: Practice & Theory*)

Legal and Ethical Issues in Acquisitions, edited by Katina Strauch and A. Bruce Strauch (No. 3, 1990). *"This excellent compilation is recommended to both collection development/acquisition librarians and library administrators in academic libraries."* (*The Journal of Academic Librarianship*)

The Acquisitions Budget, edited by Bill Katz (No. 2, 1989). *"Practical advice and tips are offered throughout . . . Those new to acquisitions work, especially in academic libraries, will find the book useful background reading."* (*Library Association Record*)

Automated Acquisitions: Issues for the Present and Future, edited by Amy Dykeman (No. 1, 1989). *"This book should help librarians to learn from the experience of colleagues in choosing the system that best suits their local requirements . . . [It] will appeal to library managers as well as to library school faculty and students."* (*Library Association Record*)

Collection Development Policies: New Directions for Changing Collections

Daniel C. Mack
Editor

Collection Development Policies: New Directions for Changing Collections has been co-published simultaneously as *The Acquisitions Librarian,* Number 30 2003.

The Haworth Information Press®
An Imprint of The Haworth Press, Inc.

New York • London • Victoria (AU)
www.HaworthPress.com

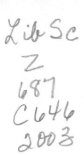

Lib Sc
Z
687
C646
2003

Published by

The Haworth Information Press®, 10 Alice Street, Binghamton, NY 13904-1580 USA

The Haworth Information Press® is an imprint of The Haworth Press, Inc., 10 Alice Street, Binghamton, NY 13904-1580 USA.

Collection Development Policies: New Directions for Changing Collections has been co-published simultaneously as *The Acquisitions Librarian*™, Number 30 2003.

© 2003 by The Haworth Press, Inc. All rights reserved. No part of this work may be reproduced or utilized in any form or by any means, electronic or mechanical, including photocopying, microfilm and recording, or by any information storage and retrieval system, without permission in writing from the publisher. Printed in the United States of America.

The development, preparation, and publication of this work has been undertaken with great care. However, the publisher, employees, editors, and agents of The Haworth Press and all imprints of The Haworth Press, Inc., including The Haworth Medical Press® and The Pharmaceutical Products Press®, are not responsible for any errors contained herein or for consequences that may ensue from use of materials or information contained in this work. Opinions expressed by the author(s) are not necessarily those of The Haworth Press, Inc. With regard to case studies, identities and circumstances of individuals discussed herein have been changed to protect confidentiality. Any resemblance to actual persons, living or dead, is entirely coincidental.

Cover design by Lora Wiggins.

Library of Congress Cataloging-in-Publication Data

Collection development policies : new directions for changing collections / Daniel C. Mack.
    p. cm.
    "Co-published simultaneously as The acquisitions librarian, number 30, 2003."
    Includes bibliographical references and index.
    ISBN 0-7890-1470-X (alk. paper) – ISBN 0-7890-1471-8 (pbk. : alk. paper)
    1. Collection development (Libraries). 2. Collection development (Libraries)–Policy statements. 3. Academic libraries–Collection development. I. Mack, Daniel C. II. Acquisitions librarian.
Z687 .C646 2003
025.2′1–dc22

2003018491

Indexing, Abstracting & Website/Internet Coverage

This section provides you with a list of major indexing & abstracting services. That is to say, each service began covering this periodical during the year noted in the right column. Most Websites which are listed below have indicated that they will either post, disseminate, compile, archive, cite or alert their own Website users with research-based content from this work. (This list is as current as the copyright date of this publication.)

Abstracting, Website/Indexing Coverage . . . . Year When Coverage Began

- **CNPIEC Reference Guide: Chinese National Directory**
  of Foreign Periodicals 1996

- **Combined Health Information Database (CHID)** 1996

- **Current Cites [Digital Libraries] [Electronic Publishing]**
  [Multimedia & Hypermedia] [Networks & Networking]
  [General] 2000

- **Current Index to Journals in Education** 2002

- **Educational Administration Abstracts (EAA)** 1991

- **FRANCIS. INIST/CNRS <www.inist.fr>** 1997

- **IBZ International Bibliography of Periodical Literature**
  <www.saur.de> 1997

- **Index Guide to College Journals (core list compiled by integrating**
  48 indexes frequently used to support undergraduate programs
  in small to medium sized libraries) 1999

- **Index to Periodical Articles Related to Law** 1992

- **Information Reports & Bibliographies** 1992

- **Information Science Abstracts <www.infotoday.com>** 1992

- **Informed Librarian, The <http://www.infosourcespub.com>** 1993

(continued)

*Exact start date to come.

Special Bibliographic Notes related to special journal issues (separates) and indexing/abstracting:

- indexing/abstracting services in this list will also cover material in any "separate" that is co-published simultaneously with Haworth's special thematic journal issue or DocuSerial. Indexing/abstracting usually covers material at the article/chapter level.
- monographic co-editions are intended for either non-subscribers or libraries which intend to purchase a second copy for their circulating collections.
- monographic co-editions are reported to all jobbers/wholesalers/approval plans. The source journal is listed as the "series" to assist the prevention of duplicate purchasing in the same manner utilized for books-in-series.
- to facilitate user/access services all indexing/abstracting services are encouraged to utilize the co-indexing entry note indicated at the bottom of the first page of each article/chapter/contribution.
- this is intended to assist a library user of any reference tool (whether print, electronic, online, or CD-ROM) to locate the monographic version if the library has purchased this version but not a subscription to the source journal.
- individual articles/chapters in any Haworth publication are also available through the Haworth Document Delivery Service (HDDS).

Collection Development Policies: New Directions for Changing Collections

CONTENTS

ABOUT THE EDITOR

Daniel C. Mack, MLS, MA, is Humanities Librarian at Pennsylvania State University. He holds advanced degrees in library science and history and has nearly fifteen years of experience in library material acquisition. Mr. Mack has managed collections in a number of settings, including large universities, commuter campuses, and a maximum-security prison. He is an active member of the American Library Association, the Association of College and Research Libraries, and the Reference and User Services Association. Mr. Mack's previous publications include an article on reference sources for Islam in *Reference and User Services Quarterly* and a charter on resources for history in *The Social Sciences: A Cross-Disciplinary Guide to Selected Sources.*

∞ ALL HAWORTH INFORMATION PRESS
BOOKS AND JOURNALS ARE PRINTED
ON CERTIFIED ACID-FREE PAPER

Introduction:
Changing Collections, Changing Policies

When most people think of libraries, they think of the collections of books and other materials that comprise a library. The collection is the central point of the institution. Employees and services exist to build, maintain, and provide access to the collection. Librarians have always used various methods to maintain control of these collections. One of the most important means for doing so has been the collection development policy. Whether existing as a formal and public statement or as a vague set of rules in the back of a librarian's mind, the collection development policy has offered librarians a set of directions for regulating the content of their libraries. One major issue facing libraries is whether there ought to be a formal policy statement for collection development at all, what it ought to say, and how it should be publicized.

In the new millennium librarians face new problems. Digital and other media have their own set of rules, and often do not fall into the neat categories that librarians have traditionally established. In addition, these new formats have their own troubles regarding acquisition, archiving, pricing, and licensing. Libraries must learn to deal with these issues, and incorporate them into their collection policies.

Librarians face other concerns as well. Especially in academic and research libraries, the dissolution of disciplinary boundaries often creates problems when collections cross traditional subject boundaries. The internationalization of the curriculum has a similar effect on collection issues. Likewise, new methodologies and approaches to scholarship abound. Race, ethnic, and gender studies, feminist and queer theory, identity politics, and varieties of postmodernism and other criti-

[Haworth co-indexing entry note]: "Introduction: Changing Collections, Changing Policies." Mack, Daniel C. Co-published simultaneously in *The Acquisitions Librarian* (The Haworth Information Press, an imprint of The Haworth Press, Inc.) No. 30, 2003, pp. 1-2; and: *Collection Development Policies: New Directions for Changing Collections* (ed: Daniel C. Mack) The Haworth Information Press, an imprint of The Haworth Press, Inc., 2003, pp. 1-2. Single or multiple copies of this article are available for a fee from The Haworth Document Delivery Service [1-800-HAWORTH, 9:00 a.m. - 5:00 p.m. (EST). E-mail address: docdelivery@ haworthpress.com].

http://www.haworthpress.com/store/product.asp?sku=J101
© 2003 by The Haworth Press, Inc. All rights reserved.
10.1300/J101v15n30_01

cal theories now influence research and publishing in nearly every discipline. Librarians responsible for maintaining, evaluating, and adding to collections in all subject areas must now be much more aware of topics, methodologies, and practices from other disciplines and other geographic areas than in the past. This in turn is (or ought to be) reflected in collection development policies.

Old problems continue to have an impact on collection development policy as well. Space issues are not new to libraries, nor are they going away. Problems also surround the means and locations to archive digital materials. Budget constraints affect not only which materials to purchase, but where and how collections should be located, both physically and electronically. Trying to decide which materials to keep, for how long to keep them, and where to house these materials are all questions that libraries must answer.

Within libraries, acquisitions librarians are learning to work in new ways with their own colleagues. The bibliographers responsible for making collection development decisions must work with catalogers and other technical services staff to implement policies effectively and efficiently. Collection decisions are increasingly shared by not only the librarians responsible for acquiring materials, but by those units within the library that must catalog, process, and provide access to the collections. By collaborating with other members of the institution, acquisitions librarians are better able to ensure that their own policies fit in with the goals and objectives of the larger organization.

The contributors to this work address these and other important matters regarding collection development policies. We examine how these policies affect electronic resources, contemporary topics, curriculum materials, and other types of library resources. We also look at how specific institutions and individual subject areas have dealt with collection development issues. In addition, we consider the role of technical services units and their influence on collections decisions, and we investigate how well, or poorly, libraries publicize their policies.

Daniel C. Mack

Pricing and Acquisitions Policies for Electronic Resources: Is the Market Stable Enough to Establish Local Standards?

Rebecca S. Albitz

SUMMARY. Librarians establish pricing policies for traditional acquisitions to systematize what can be an unpredictable process. This article discusses whether the electronic resource market is currently stable enough for librarians to apply similar policies to their electronic acquisitions. It also examines the history and current state of electronic resource pricing, and relates electronic resource pricing policy preferences as articulated by professionals who work closely with electronic resource acquisitions. *[Article copies available for a fee from The Haworth Document Delivery Service: 1-800-HAWORTH. E-mail address: <docdelivery@haworthpress.com> Website: <http://www.HaworthPress.com> © 2003 by The Haworth Press, Inc. All rights reserved.]*

KEYWORDS. Electronic resources, acquisitions policies, pricing models

Rebecca S. Albitz is Electronic Resources and Copyright Librarian, The Pennsylvania State University Libraries, 327 Pattee Library, University Park, PA 16802 (E-mail: rsa4@psu.edu).

[Haworth co-indexing entry note]: "Pricing and Acquisitions Policies for Electronic Resources: Is the Market Stable Enough to Establish Local Standards?" Albitz, Rebecca S. Co-published simultaneously in *The Acquisitions Librarian* (The Haworth Information Press, an imprint of The Haworth Press, Inc.) No. 30, 2003, pp. 3-13; and: *Collection Development Policies: New Directions for Changing Collections* (ed: Daniel C. Mack) The Haworth Information Press, an imprint of The Haworth Press, Inc., 2003, pp. 3-13. Single or multiple copies of this article are available for a fee from The Haworth Document Delivery Service [1-800-HAWORTH, 9:00 a.m. - 5:00 p.m. (EST). E-mail address: docdelivery@haworthpress.com].

http://www.haworthpress.com/store/product.asp?sku=J101
© 2003 by The Haworth Press, Inc. All rights reserved.
10.1300/J101v15n30_02

INTRODUCTION

When customers or libraries buy books, they follow a well-defined process. The customer may walk into a bookstore or log onto Amazon.com, select a title of interest, and pay the price on the book jacket or computer screen. An acquiring librarian may also adopt either of these two strategies, finding little or no pricing ambiguity. Even when bookstores, online book dealers, and book jobbers offer volume or club member discounts, book prices rarely pose a mystery for the purchaser. When, however, a library negotiates access to an electronic resource, it rarely finds the same transparency. Because so many pricing structures exist in the electronic resources arena, a licensee often finds it difficult to determine how the vendor determines a price and why that vendor has chosen one pricing model over another. This uncertainty complicates the already confused process of licensing electronic information for the academic community. What many librarians desire, as a result, is electronic resource pricing as predictable and budgetable as the pricing for monographs and serials.

For acquiring these established, traditional library resource formats, librarians have been able to establish polices that guide how much they pay and to whom they make payment. They have also set parameters for approval plans, limiting the receipt of monographs priced over a certain amount. They systematically review serials titles to determine the relative value of a title as compared to its subscription cost. The question is whether these approaches will ever be possible for electronic resources. Accordingly, this article discusses some early pricing models the electronic resources vendor community adopted before the acceptance of the World Wide Web as the primary delivery mechanism. Then it examines current pricing structures for both electronic indexing and aggregator products and for electronic journals. Finally, the author asked librarians familiar with electronic resource issues to discuss pricing structures they find suitable for their institutions and for varying types of resources, indicating perhaps that individual institutions might be able to establish local acquisitions policies governing electronic resources budgeting.

EARLY ELECTRONIC RESOURCE PRICING MODELS

Online Resources

Information provider pricing models have posed problems in academic libraries since online databases became fixtures there during the early 1980s. The technology used to access most electronic, or online, resources in the 1980s and early 1990s required one to use a telephone connection to dial into a vendor's database. This type of access shaped how information providers configured pricing at that time. In her introduction to a series of interviews conducted with electronic resource vendors, Eileen Abels (1996) described the pricing options available during the early days of electronic resource access, which included "connect time, flat fee per search, computer resources, subscription or flat fee-pricing per year, and differential by time of day."[1] Ables also found that many vendors based their pricing on the type of client they served. Academic institutions might receive one rate, while a business or law firm needing highly specialized information might be charged another, and a high-use research company might be charged a third rate. At the time when she conducted her interviews, Abels found librarians, primarily, mediating the searches in those products available in order to minimize costs, since the expert searcher presumably had the knowledge to conduct clean, quick, focused searches and minimize connect time. Another pricing model vendors applied in this early online environment, where connect time determined much of the pricing, was called "port pricing," or an annual flat rate for access to a system. While this model now reflects the majority of current vendor billing models, it was unusual in the early 1990s and was sometimes implemented unethically. Questel-Orbit's, Inc.'s Mike Wilkes described this model as follows:

> There has been a tendency by some of the vendors to turn off the clock during the first period, giving the service to the user at a very low rate–'$500 a month for unlimited access to our service.' So they hook you. You get used to going online at the drop of a hat and you pay only $500.00 per month. At the end of the 12-month period, that vendor comes to you and says, 'You only spent $6,000.00 in cash with us [12 × $500.00] but you really used $15,000.00 worth of information. If you want to continue on this plan next year, it will now cost a minimum of $15,000.00.'[2]

One still occasionally finds this type of bait-and-switch pricing, although its contemporary iteration tends to begin as a "free with print" model, which will be discussed later.

CD-ROM Pricing

As technologies have changed, so have pricing models. Bill O'Conor, from Disclosure, Inc. observed back in 1995 that "most of the online vendors have adjusted, as we have, to the new technology realities, though the pricing model of time connected is under extreme pressure as baud rates increase."[3] Internet speed affected pricing, and so did the development and wide adoption of the CD-ROM. CD-ROMs allowed a researcher to conduct literature searches without the mediation of a librarian or other information professional. Self-searching provided flexibility, invited experimentation, and allowed for mistakes, whereas online searching penalized a searcher interested in browsing the literature rather than conducting focused searches. O'Conor, of Disclosure, Inc. also stated that the primary pricing strategy the CD-ROM imposed on online services was the "all-you-can-eat fixed price, which put pricing pressure on the online services, especially for big users. CD-ROMs offered a more economical way to retrieve large quantities of data."[4] By virtue of its physical format, and by its single-user limitation–before the development of local area networks, or LANs–the CD-ROM invites more book-like pricing: the librarian pays a one-time price to purchase a physical object, rather than licensing access to a remote database.

CURRENT PRICING FOR ELECTRONIC RESOURCES

Electronic Journals

The advent of broad, inexpensive access to the Internet has, of course, revolutionized access to electronic information resources, and the Internet has also had a powerful impact on electronic resource vendor pricing models. While neither mediated searching (paying by connect time or result sets) nor CD-ROMs (paying primarily for a single user, full access product) have gone away, Web-based networked access to electronic resources has superseded them. The variety of information resources now available electronically–full-text journals, encyclopedias, indices, and data sets, for example–is surpassed only by the variety of ways a library can pay for these resources. In fact, so many different pricing models exist that one finds it nearly impossible to understand them all. In fact, as Hardy, Oppenheim, and Rubbert (2002) state, "The greatest enigma in the online world remains pricing."[5] The goal for publishers, of course, is to maintain or increase their profits while providing a quality product, and the goal of librarians is to provide the resources likeliest to facilitate teaching and learning while adhering to a budget. Unfortunately, according to The International Coalition of Library Consortia's (ICOLC) "Statement of Current Perspectives and Preferred Practices for the Selection and Purchase of Electronic

Information" (1998) academic institutions and library clients "expect their libraries to obtain new electronic resources while simultaneously maintaining or growing traditional collections."[6]

This expectation is particularly true of serials where collections growth can become unsustainable in an economic climate where budget increases, if they occur at all, fail to meet the rate of print subscription inflation. Spending limited funds to acquire electronic access to information duplicated in a print collection can hardly be sustained over an extended period and are, therefore, difficult to justify to university administrations. The ICOLC statement continues: "Academic libraries cannot afford to commit long-term to the now prevalent electronic journal pricing model that is premised upon a base price of 'current print price plus electronic surcharge *plus* significant projected inflation surcharges.' "[7] Several electronic journal publishers now offer the Print-plus-a-percentage-for-electronic-access model. But other pricing models are also being applied to electronic journal titles and to journal packages. Some electronic journal publishers offer the reverse option for their clients–that is, charging a flat subscription rate for the electronic version of a journal and adding a surcharge to maintain the print subscription. Other electronic journal package providers, however, have decoupled their electronic pricing from their print pricing, allowing a subscriber to choose either a paper or electronic format for the same base price, and offering access to both for an additional surcharge over the initial price. Finally, some publishers still offer the electronic version of their journals free with a print subscription. While with this arrangement, access remains tied to the print format, no additional charges accrue to libraries for multiple versions of the same information.

Electronic Aggregators and Indices

Tying electronic pricing to print subscriptions currently appears to be the pricing model most often employed by electronic journal vendors. For such other electronic resources as online indices, e-books, aggregator products and databases, a variety of other pricing models exist. Two of the most common ones are based on institutional fulltime equivalents (FTEs) and concurrent users. Each of these models has advantages and disadvantages that depend on the nature of the product and the size and type of the institutional subscriber. The products most suited to a concurrent user model are those that are highly specialized–that is to say, the potential user base is small relative to the size of the licensing institution as a whole. One disadvantage becomes apparent, however, when one tries to conduct bibliographic instruction in a hands-on setting utilizing a product licensed for a limited number of users. On occasion, pricing for a highly specialized product can seem completely disproportionate to the small number of licensed concurrent users. One reason might be that the universe of potential licensors is so small that, in order for vendors to recover production and maintenance costs, they must charge a relatively high fee for the product. In order to justify the expenditure, an individual institution would have to weigh the cost of the product against its usefulness to its community.

FTE-based pricing can also be applied to both general interest databases and subject-based products. If, in fact, a large portion of an institution's population might access a resource, then FTE-based pricing could make sense. It allows a large number of users to access a database at the same time, and it also allows large library instruction classes, or participants in multiple bibliographic sessions, to access the same resource at the same time. If, however, an information provider bases the cost of a specialized product license on an institution's FTE, issues of inequity arise. A large institution would certainly be reluctant to pay for a product with a price based on 60,000 FTEs, when the potential user population consisted of perhaps thirty people. In these situations some information providers base their pricing not on an institution's entire FTE, but on the FTEs affiliated with a program or programs with a user population likely to need this specialized data. While these numbers can be difficult to ascertain, particularly at a large research institution, this model is certainly more equitable and sustainable than the alternative.

Pricing Model Anomalies and Issues

Having considered the most commonly applied pricing models information providers currently offer, one should also realize that a number of more unusual models exist. Three of these anomalies include pricing based on Carnegie classification, degrees granted in a particular field, and number of Internet Protocol, or IP, addresses that will be authorized to access the product. These models, and others like them, may appeal to certain licensing institutions, depending on their size and user needs. Such e-book collections as netLibrary and Safari offer other pricing models. Because netLibrary's collection has a potentially long shelf life, it offers an actual book purchasing model where a library purchases access to the book in perpetuity. Or, if the library chooses, it can lease access for a certain length of time. Because Safari's collection contains such disposable titles as computer software manuals, its pricing is not based on a permanent acquisitions model but on a matrix of concurrent users and "points." Each of the books in its collection is assigned a point value. A library determines how many points it wants to pay for and how many concurrent users it needs to satisfy demand for the product. These two factors determine the cost of the package. (This model is so new that its usefulness has yet to be evaluated.)

One factor that tends to complicate many pricing models is the definition of a "site." Some information providers seek to base their pricing on some combination of FTE or concurrent user and the number of physical "sites" associated with an institution. One commonly finds two definitions of a site. The first is geographic–that is, users have to be at locations within, say, five miles of the licensing institution. The second is administrative–that is, all locations administered by the licensing institution are considered part of its site. Some licenses do not define a site at all; they create usage parameters according to their definition of an authorized user. One frequently finds a physical site restriction in licenses for free access to electronic journals with a print subscription. For small, single-site institutions, geographic site definitions rarely become an issue. Their physical plant is usually compact, and their research facilities are usually located on the campus. In larger institutions, however, a site restriction can keep the institution from licensing access to resources, because the institution has multiple campus locations or research facilities located outside of the main campus. This problem becomes exacerbated by the fact that IP ranges cannot be geographically segregated if they are randomly distributed throughout all the institution's locations. Ironically, the inclusion of such a site restriction in a license has become archaic, with the widespread use of proxy servers that permit remote access to electronic resources. The physical location of the user is no longer an access issue, and it should no longer influence product pricing.

PRICING MODEL PREFERENCES

Information providers and librarians can hardly dispute the fact that we currently find ourselves in a state of electronic resource chaos. Libraries find it difficult to pay for both print and electronic versions of the same resources, and information providers must remain accountable to their shareholders while sustaining parallel forms of information production. Moreover, as Hardy, Oppenheim and Rubbert (2002) concluded, no single reliable solution presents itself: "The economics of digital library services are characterized by fluidity, making it unlikely that a static model will be appropriate during the evolution of this young market."[8] This fluidity means that sellers apply different models to different products depending upon their decision to adopt the pricing model they consider most cost effective for their product. The question becomes whether librarians consider these pricing structures to be well-suited for specific products and certain sizes of institutions, and whether librarians can base their acquisitions policies on the models best suited to their needs.

To address and clarify this marketplace issue, the author addressed a series of questions to the participants of ERIL-l (electronic resources in libraries listserv) on September 26, 2002. While the number of responses was low, the comments provided useful insights. List subscribers were asked what pricing model they preferred for both general and specialized indexing and aggregator products. For general interest products respondents from larger institutions (10,000+ FTE) primarily preferred FTE pricing or pricing based on the size of the institution. This response is logical since a greater chance exists that a large portion of a large population would be inclined to use such a product. For specialized databases, the larger institutions preferred a concurrent user model, as reduced demand for the product would be expected. But two exceptions to these preferences are of interest. One institutional representative said he preferred FTE pricing for specialized databases if the FTE count included only those persons most likely to use the product. Another respondent preferred FTE pricing for all products because the librarians "hated to get busy signals," indicating that all their electronic seats were currently occupied. Respondents from smaller institutions (under 1,500 FTE) preferred FTE-based pricing for all indexing and aggregator products. No representative from an institution with an FTE between 1,500 and 10,000 responded to these questions, but one might extrapolate that their responses would include preferences for both pricing models depending on the type of product they were considering.

The author also posed two questions about preferred pricing structures for electronic journals. The first sought the preferred pricing configuration for electronic access if the institution already had a print subscription. Half of the eight responses indicated that they preferred to pay a percentage over the print cost for electronic access. Three responded that they prefer the pricing for electronic access to remain completely separate from print subscriptions. One person preferred the electronic access costs to be the primary cost and a print subscription to be a percentage of the electronic access cost. The second question centered on how the respondents would prefer to pay if their institutions did not already have a print subscription. Five advocated access to the electronic version of a journal without having a print copy and wanted this pricing to remain separate from print costs. Two believed the electronic access cost should be the base cost and a print subscription should be a percentage over the base price. Two respondents specifically mentioned an expectation that the price for the electronic access-only model be lower than the cost for a print subscription.

Finally, the author asked all eight colleagues whether they believed that one ideal pricing model might prove equitable for both information providers and libraries, but no consensus emerged. One respondent considered FTE pricing to be the most equitable. Another agreed, but wanted to base FTE on the actual user community for a specific product rather than for the entire institution. Two other similar responses suggested that pricing models should be based on actual usage. A base price would be established, and usage data would determine additional costs–not unlike the pricing models employed when electronic resources were available solely through mediated searching. The remaining four concluded that no ideal pricing model currently exists and that flexibility is necessary because no one model is appropriate for every institution or every product.

Although a limited number of ERIL-l participants responded to the posed questions, the perspectives of those who did respond mirror those held by their colleagues as set forth in the article entitled "Electronic Pubs Pricing in the Web Era."[9] Knight and Hillson (1998) summarized there the pros and cons of a number of different pricing models identified during the 1998 North American Serials Interest Group (NASIG) conference. Among the sixteen pricing models the NASIG workshop participants identified were those mentioned in the ERIL-l responses discussed here, and the pros and cons in that article closely reflect the same comments the later discussion elicited. The strongly positive response to an FTE-based model, or "sliding scale" model as Knight and Hillson call it, reflects the appearance of equity it embodies–that is, the larger the user base, the more one pays. Yet, as the Knight and Hillson article and some of the e-mail respondents indicated, a user population is often a subset of the entire institutional population. The concurrent or simultaneous user model allows libraries to pay for the number of users who might be interested in the product, and information providers can predict the load level on their system. Unfortunately, one disadvantage is that this model can "limit access to information at peak usage times if simultaneous access is inaccurately defined."[10] Another drawback, as mentioned earlier, is the inability to conduct a hands-on instructional session with products that admit only a few concurrent users.

Knight and Hillson also addressed electronic journal pricing models and found that the positive aspects of the model featuring a print format plus a surcharge for electronic access included providing access to remote users and a low administrative burden. These advantages pertain if print prices and inflation rates remain stable–which, unfortunately, tends not to be the case. Problems with this model include paying for the same information twice and linking electronic access to a print subscription, which does not allow the subscribing library to cancel the print version while keeping its electronic access. The electronic-plus-an-additional-cost-for-print model provides print cancellation flexibility, but the issues of perpetual archival access and product stability become compelling. One model intentionally excluded from the e-mail discussion at hand but addressed in the Knight and Hillson article is free electronic access with a print subscription, a highly valued service for those institutions where the various site restrictions discussed earlier do not apply. As we also saw earlier, and as the NASIG participants stated, however, the major concern surrounding this model is the "addiction strategy" some vendors employ. Such vendors "create a market for a publication that might become cost prohibitive in the future, when it is no longer free."[11] A number of information providers have recently begun to charge for access, providing little warning to their current customers and creating public relations nightmares for librarians forced to explain budget constraints to irate patrons.

CONCLUSION

As one examines the brief and volatile history of electronic information resources, it becomes apparent that an ideal pricing model has yet to emerge. For some institutions, mandating policies that electronic resources pricing conform to specific patterns may hold a certain amount of appeal, particularly for small institutions that require only a limited number of electronic resources. For example, an FTE-based pricing model might accommodate both general interest and highly specialized products. But for larger institutions, such a policy might either limit the number of users who could access a product with wide appeal, causing endless access complaints, or require large financial outlays for highly specialized products of limited user interest.

Establishing pricing model policies for electronic journal subscriptions is, however, certainly possible, and in some cases highly desirable. As the purchasing power of acquisitions budgets falls, some institutions have begun to establish "electronic only" journal policies, and even if print is available for a surcharge, these institutions license access only to the electronic version. This strategy eliminates content duplication and also addresses restricted space issues. Another policy option is to refuse to link to any "free with print" electronic journal. While some users would reject this decision, a librarian might conclude that providing access and then having to remove it would result in more negative publicity than not linking to it at all. Prudent librarians will establish such policies if they believe that the resulting budget, collection management, and administrative benefits outweigh the potential public relations problems resulting from an inability to provide access to a product because some vendor refuses to work with them.

NOTES

1. Eileen G. Ables, "Pricing of Electronic Resources: Interviews with Three Vendors," *Journal of the American Society for Information Science* 47 n.3(1996): 235.

2. Abels, 240.

3. Abels, 237.

4. Abels, 237.

5. Rachel Hardy, Charles Oppenheim and Iris Rubbert, "Pricing Strategies and Models for the Provision of Digitized Texts in Higher Education," *Journal of Information Science* 28 n.2(2002): 98.

6. International Coalition of Library Consortia (ICOLC), Statement of Current Perspective and Preferred Practices for the Selection and Purchase of Electronic Information, 25 March 1998, www.yale.edu/consortia/statement.html (30 September 2002).

7. ICOLC.

8. Hardy, 100.

9. Nancy H. Knight and Susan B. Hillson, "Electronic Pubs Pricing in the Web Era," *Information Today* 15 n.8(September 1998).

10. Knight, 40.

11. Knight, 39.

Subject-Specific Policy Statements:
A Rationale and Framework
for Collection Development

Glenn S. McGuigan
Gary W. White

SUMMARY. Traditional collection development policy statements are broad documents intended for entire libraries or based upon certain formats or certain audience characteristics. Subject-specific policy statements are an alternative form that can be used to more clearly delineate the scope and goals of particular collections. A more detailed subject-based policy better communicates the unique characteristics of a particular collection; better assists librarians who use the collection; and aids patrons who are using collections for particular research needs. Development of the subject-based policy provides an opportunity to closely analyze the present state of collections, to examine the interests and needs of clientele, and to strategically plan the future of the collection. *[Article copies available for a fee from The Haworth Document Delivery Service: 1-800-HAWORTH. E-mail address: <docdelivery@haworthpress.com> Website: <http://www.HaworthPress.com> © 2003 by The Haworth Press, Inc. All rights reserved.]*

Glenn S. McGuigan is Business Reference Librarian, The Pennsylvania State Harrisburg Library, 351 Olmsted Drive, Middletown, PA 17057-4850 (E-mail: gxm22@ psulias.psu.edu). Gary W. White is Head, Shreyer Business Library, The Pennsylvania State University Libraries, 309 Paterno Library, University Park, PA 16802 (E-mail: gww2@psulias.psu.edu).

[Haworth co-indexing entry note]: "Subject-Specific Policy Statements: A Rationale and Framework for Collection Development." McGuigan, Glenn S., and Gary W. White. Co-published simultaneously in *The Acquisitions Librarian* (The Haworth Information Press, an imprint of The Haworth Press, Inc.) No. 30, 2003, pp.15-32; and: *Collection Development Policies: New Directions for Changing Collections* (ed: Daniel C. Mack) The Haworth Information Press, an imprint of The Haworth Press, Inc., 2003, pp. 15-32. Single or multiple copies of this article are available for a fee from The Haworth Document Delivery Service [1-800-HAWORTH, 9:00 a.m. - 5:00 p.m. (EST). E-mail address: docdelivery@haworthpress.com].

http://www.haworthpress.com/store/product.asp?sku=J101
© 2003 by The Haworth Press, Inc. All rights reserved.

10.1300/J101v15n30_03

KEYWORDS. Collection development policies, subject-specific collections development policies, policy development

The use of collection development policy statements has long been a standard practice in all types of libraries. The American Library Association (ALA) defines collection policy statements as documents that define the scope of a library's existing collections, plan for the further development of resources, identify the strengths of collections, and describe the institution's selection philosophy, goals, and criteria.[1] The Collection Development Policies Committee of the Collection Development and Evaluation Section of the Reference and Adult Services Division (now the Reference and User Services Association) of ALA describes collection statements as "essential requisites to effective access and quality in collections developed and managed to support libraries' mission."[2]

The importance of collection development policy statements is evident. Johnson states that libraries without collections policy statements are akin to businesses without a business plan.[3] Are traditional policies relevant in today's digitally-oriented libraries? The Collection Development Policies Committee in 1993 stated that the traditional collection policy statements are based on ownership of material. Because of changing technologies, libraries will rely less on acquiring and storing materials and more on providing access to information through commercial vendors and cooperative programs.[4] As the scope and definition of library collections evolve, policy statements also need to evolve to address these issues.

An alternative to broad traditional collections policies or those based on format is to develop policies based on subject area. While traditional and format-based policies are still useful, more specific subject-based policies can more clearly delineate the scope and goals of particular collections.

LITERATURE REVIEW

The literature on subject-specific collection development statements is rather slim. Power and Pavy published a 1995 article on collection development in the field of communication studies. In this article, they describe the development of a "subject-special" policy as a tool to handle the two difficult tasks of collection development in a multidimensional discipline and working collegially with teaching faculty. The authors found that the process of researching and articulating the policy, including a careful analysis of collections and the research and teaching needs of communications faculty, was as important as the finished written policy.[5]

In 1995, Hazen wrote that traditional collection development (i.e., print) policies were static and did not meet the needs of librarians in the information age. He suggests the use of flexible descriptors or guides within fields of study that include all formats and local and remote resources.[6] Case agrees with Hazen in a 2000 article addressing collection development policies and humanities electronic texts. He argues that e-texts are of such importance to teaching and scholarship that librarians should not limit their selection based on "traditional artificial methods."[7]

Lein wrote a 1987 article discussing suggestions for developing collection development policy statements for music score collections. He suggests that music bibliographers use a combination of guidelines developed by what was formerly the Collection Development Committee of the Resources and Technical Services of the American Library Association and those developed by the Research Libraries Group. He finds that policy statements for music scores must be coordinated with sound recordings and the written literature on music. Lein's article thus addresses both subject and format.[8]

There are numerous articles discussing collections policies that are format based. During the 1990s there were a number of articles addressing collection development policies and electronic resources. Strong published a 1999 article offering advice on incorporating electronic resources into collection development policies. He includes a policy statement that outlines the order of preference for print and electronic formats.[9] Vogel also published a 1996 article outlining the integration of electronic resources into print collection policy statements. She advocates this integration as a necessary tool to avoid the "haphazard unfocused groupings of resources that may or may not support the mission of the library."[10] LaGuardia and Bentley addressed this subject earlier in a 1992 article in which they state that existing collection development policies are not adequate for the acquisition of datafiles. Two other articles from the late 1980s examined CD-ROMs and collections policies.[12,13]

Johnson published a 1998 column outlining the elements of distinct collection development policies for electronic resources. She advocates that they, like print collections policies, follow a standard format. She offers guidelines for the selection of electronic resources as well as comparisons with the uses and benefits of print collections policies.[14] White and Crawford, in a 1997 article, described the process for developing an electronic information resources collection development policy at their institution. They recommend guidelines for selection of such resources based on relevance, potential use, demand, ease of use, availability to multiple users, stability of coverage, longevity, price and predictability of price, equipment needs, and available technical support.[15]

There are many works addressing the uses and importance of collection policy statements and on the process of creating collection policies. Johnson writes that policies describe current collections, assist with budgeting, establish priorities, serve as a communications link between the library and its constituents, support cooperative collection development, protect intellectual freedom, and assist with gifts, deselection, and cancellations.[16] Intner describes them as long range strategic plans that are the best tools for shaping collections that match the needs of users.[17] The process of developing a policy is addressed in a 1991 article written by Cassell and Futas.[18] Futas also published a work containing examples of collection policy statements from various institutions.[19]

THE RATIONALE FOR SUBJECT SPECIFIC POLICY STATEMENTS

Subject-specific policy statements clearly articulate the state and the level of subject collections and may be used for a variety of collection development activities. Serving as measurement tools indicating the currency of materials and the depth of coverage of a particular collection, these documents communicate the institution's collection development policy concerning the acquisition and retention of materials within a particular subject area. Subject-specific policy statements assist users who benefit from an accurate description of the scope of a collection, as well as those responsible for maintaining and developing collections, by providing a descriptive assessment upon which to base collection development decisions. For training purposes, these documents serve as a useful educational tool for library science students and practitioners.

These specific policy statements serve users better than generic or general statements. While general or generic statements deliver only a vague indication of the scope of a collection, subject specific policy statements, by providing more specificity, communicate the unique characteristics of a particular collection. By presenting a detailed level of description of the content of the collection, these documents aid users who benefit by being able to determine the appropriate scope of a collection for a particular research need. A clear statement of the policies regulating use of the materials within the collection also assists users by eliminating any ambiguity regarding restrictions or limitations on access.

Subject specific policy statements are more specific than format-based statements and audience (i.e., age, educational level) based statements. Format-based statements, by identifying materials based solely upon material-type, often do not adequately reflect the diverse content of most collections that consist of various types of media. These statements also may not address issues relating to the duplication of materials found in both paper and electronic formats. Audience based statements, on the other hand, provide information regarding the level of a certain collection based upon the characteristics of a particular user group. By focusing only upon the user population as the single measurement tool, audience based statements may not provide specific details about the collection. By providing a measurement of a collection based solely upon one set of criteria, these statements often deliver a one-dimensional view of the contents of a collection.

DEVELOPMENT OF THE POLICY

The development of subject specific policy statements consists of four phases of analysis addressing the most critical topics regarding the qualities and use of a collection. Issues to be analyzed in the development of the policy include: the present state of the collection; the relevant programs/courses that the library supports; the interests and needs of the clientele; and the impact of cooperative agreements. The topics of these stages of analysis construct the criteria upon which the policy statement is formed.

Analyzing the present state of the collection marks the first step in the development of the policy. This activity serves as a collection development maintenance exercise by examining the strengths and weaknesses, the scope and the depth, of a particular collection. Points that may be addressed in this review include the description of electronic indexing or abstracting services and other databases that are currently licensed for use by the institution, number of monographs and periodicals, and the currency of the materials.

An analysis of the relevant programs and courses that the library supports addresses the primary mission of the academic library in supporting the curriculum of the institution. Actions that may be undertaken within this process include summarizing the research requirements of each degree offered by the particular department or program and describing the scope of particular courses, especially those with a primary research focus, that the library is supporting. This activity forges a direct link between the subject collection and the academic program that utilizes these resources. In public libraries, an analysis of community programs and other needs of local citizens is necessary.

Analysis of the clientele of the library is an important component in the development of the policy statement. Relating to the mission of the institution in supporting the needs of the library's constituents, factors that may be addressed in analyzing the clientele include faculty research interests, the needs of students, and the role of the library in providing service to the public.

Depending upon the acquisition policy of the library, faculty research interests may propel the collection of highly specific and in-depth scholarly material suitable for a research library collection. This analysis provides the opportunity for collaboration with teaching faculty in order to identify specific research interests and needs and to examine how the library's collection of resources meets those needs.

As students form the primary constituency of a library, their needs are met by focusing upon the acquisition of materials that will support course-related research activity. Other factors may be taken into consideration in this analysis such as the need for information focusing upon academic or career development, technology skill acquisition or health related matters.

Determined by the mission of the institution, service to the public, as a segment of the collection development policy, may be addressed by focusing upon materials that will serve the interests of the local community. This could include analyzing the need for materials such as medical, legal or community information resources as well as recreational materials. In public libraries, outreach to the local community is the obvious mission.

The impact of cooperative agreements may be included in the policy statement if they affect collection development decisions for the subject area. Reciprocal borrowing agreements between institutions, consortia database licensing agreements, and agreements with other subject areas may be analyzed in order to determine the impact of these agreements upon the collection development policy.

ITEMS TO INCLUDE IN THE SUBJECT-SPECIFIC POLICY STATEMENT

Within the subject-specific policy statement, the following items should be included in order to provide the most complete description of the collection and of the policy regarding acquisition and retention of materials.

- *Names/Contact Information of Selectors*–includes titles and specific collection development subject expertise of the selectors within the particular discipline.
- *Statement of Purpose*–provides an explanation of the needs of users and how the library, through the statement of this policy, proposes to meet those needs. This statement should summarize the goal or plan of the policy.
- *Introduction to the Collection*–delivers a broad overview of the collection in terms of subject matter and material collected; indicates where the collection is physically located. Introductory section broadly describes clientele and their needs. This introduction may relate the history of the collection and particular strengths or unique features of the collection.
- *Programmatic Information*–communicates the nature of the academic programs, including the particular degrees that are offered by each program supported by the library. This information connects the collection to the specific curricular needs of the institution. In public libraries, this may include library based programs such as adult literacy or after school student help sessions.
- *Coordination of Collections*–identifies administrator or librarian responsible for coordinating selection; may identify selector who is responsible for collecting in the appropriate subject area.
- *Cooperative Information*–relates how the subject collection may intersect with other collections within the library and with other libraries. This segment may discuss any cooperative agreements, such as reciprocal borrowing or consortia database licensing agreements, with other libraries. Delivers explanation of any cooperative collection development activity.
- *Modifiers*–transmits the parameters of the collection by subject, language, format, and geographic location; relates the various formats found within a collection. This section communicates specific types of items that are specifically selected or excluded based upon format.
- *Description of Materials Collected*–describes the nature of materials collected. Includes:

  - Location of the materials–relays the physical location of print materials and other in-house items and states the types of electronic resources available.
  - Levels/intensity of the collections–describes the depth of resources within a collection.

- Currency of materials/guidance on retention–relates the policy on currency of various materials and delivers guidelines on retaining materials.
- Quality of materials–assesses the quality of the resources within the collection and establishes standards for measuring the level of quality.
- Statement on the duplication of materials–establishes guidelines on when duplication of content may take place.
- Limitations on the use of collections–addresses any issues regarding limitations on access.
- Institution-specific considerations/policies–describes any special policies or issues that concern a specific institution.
- Legal/regulatory restrictions on use of the collection–alerts users to any specific legal restrictions.

Other items can and should be included if they are germane to the subject area. There is a need to strike an appropriate balance of specificity. Subject collection policy statements that are too vague will do little to guide selection. Those that are too narrow have the potential to limit new directions that the subject area may take and therefore may necessitate frequent updating.

USES OF THE POLICY

Collection development policies are meant to be tools to aid librarians and library users. They are of little value if they are merely written and not used to assist selectors or are not promoted. Well-written policies serve a variety of intra- and external institutional purposes. Internally, subject-specific policy statements serve to guide selectors and to provide information to administrators. In larger organizations, they provide information to other librarians about the scope of collections. This is especially important because of the interdisciplinary nature of most subjects.

Crafting the policy statement serves as a tool for understanding the present state of collections, an advantage well-documented in the literature. This exercise also serves as a springboard for determining future goals for the organization. Thus, subject policy statements also serve as an important strategic planning tool.

Another valuable application is to use policy statements as a training tool. Exposing new employees to the present state of subject collections, the philosophy and mission of the library in terms of its collections, and a description of the audience and scope of collections will provide them with important information about the collections. This understanding is especially important for those with collection development responsibilities and they will also serve to orient all new employees to the library.

Subject-specific policy statements are also useful when it is necessary to measure the depth and quality of collections, as in accreditation renewals or when describing collections to other libraries. In a sense, when used this way, they also serve the traditional uses of explaining and justifying collections. In these instances, it is more effective to use them in conjunction with other types of collections policies, such as those that are format-based. Another example of an extra-institutional use is to use it as a promotional tool to attract new users. While the policy statement as written probably would not be used, elements of the statement are useful when preparing promotional and marketing materials. Related examples include using elements of the policy when exploring development opportunities, preparing grants, or writing gift policies.

CONCLUSION

The importance of collection development policy statements is well-documented in the literature of librarianship. While most policies are general or format-based, the subject-specific policy statement offers many distinct advantages. There are common elements in each of these types of policy statements, but subject-specific statements provide greater specificity and better communicate the unique characteristics of a particular collection. Appendix A and B are examples of subject-specific policy statements in use at The Pennsylvania State University.

NOTES

1. American Library Association, *Guide for Writing a Bibliographer's Manual*, Chicago: American Library Association, 1987, pp. 2-3.
2. Collection Development Policies Committee, Collection Development and Evaluation Section, Reference and Adult Services Division, American Library Association, *The Relevance of Collection Development Policies: Definition, Necessity, and Applications*, RQ 33, Fall 1993, p. 65.
3. Peggy Johnson, *Collection Development Policies: A Cunning Plan*, Technicalities 14, June 1994, pp. 3-6.

4. Collection Development Policies Committee, p. 68.

5. Ann T. Power and Jeanne Pavy, *Collection Development in the Field of Communication Studies*, Collection Building 14 (1995), pp. 9-23.

6. Dan C. Hazen, *Collection Development Policies in the Information Age*, College & Research Libraries 56 (January 1995), pp. 29-31.

7. Beau David Case, *Love's Labour's Lost: The Failure of Traditional Selection Practice in the Acquisition of Humanities Electronic Texts*, Library Trends 48 (Spring 2000), pp. 729-747.

8. Edward Lein, *Suggestions for Formulating Collection Development Policy Statements for Music Score Collections in Academic Libraries*, Collection Management 9 (Winter, 1987), pp. 69-101.

9. Rob Strong, *A Collection Development Policy Incorporating Electronic Formats*, Journal of Interlibrary Loan, Document Delivery & Information Supply 9 (1999), pp. 53-64.

10. Kristin D. Vogel, *Integrating Electronic Resources into Collection Development Policies*, Collection Management 21 (1996), pp. 65-76.

11. Cheryl LaGuardia and Stella Bentley, *Electronic Databases: Will Old Collection Development Policies Still Work?* Online 16 (July 1992), pp. 60-63.

12. Anthony W. Ferguson, *Assessing the Collection Development Need for CD-ROM Products*, Library Acquisitions: Practice and Theory 12 (1988), pp. 325-332.

13. Charlene York, *Optical Disk Products in the Collection Development Policy*, CD-ROM Librarian 3 (September 1988), pp. 16-18.

14. Peggy Johnson, *Collection Policies for Electronic Resources,* Technicalities 18 (June 1998), pp. 10-12.

15. Gary W. White and Gregory A. Crawford, *Developing an Electronic Information Resources Collection Development Policy*, Collection Building 16 (1997), pp. 53-57.

16. Peggy Johnson, 1994.

17. Sheila S. Intner, *The Ostrich Syndrome: Why Written Collection Development Polices are Important*, Technicalities 16 (July/August, 1996), pp: 1, 9-10.

18. Kay Ann Cassell and Elizabeth Futas, *Collection Development Policies*, Collection Building 11 (1991), pp. 26-29.

19. Elizabeth Futas, *Collection Development Policies and Procedures*, 3rd ed. Phoenix: Oryx Press, 1995.

APPENDIX A

COLLECTION DEVELOPMENT POLICY
Schreyer Business Library
The Pennsylvania State University

PRINCIPAL SELECTORS:

Gary White	Diane Zabel	Kevin Harwell
309 Paterno	309 Paterno	309 Paterno
865-9268	865-1013	865-0141

GENERAL STATEMENT

The purpose of this selection policy is to provide the framework for obtaining material to support the Smeal College of Business Administration; the School of Hotel, Restaurant, and Recreation Management; the Department of Economics; and business and business-related programs throughout the University. This policy statement is intended to be flexible and subject to frequent evaluations.

INTRODUCTION TO THE COLLECTION

The Schreyer Business Library is located on the third floor of the Paterno Library. Additional materials are also located in the Microforms Department on the ground floor of the Pattee Library. The collection provides support for all undergraduate, graduate, and doctoral programs offered at the University, including the distance education Master of Business Administration program. The Schreyer Business Library, while collecting in all areas of business administration and economics, has strong collections in U.S. and international company information; hospitality and tourism; career information; and entrepreneurship. In addition, the Schreyer Business Library is a U.S. Patent and Trademark Depository Library.

PROGRAM INFORMATION

The Schreyer Business Library supports approximately 8,000 undergraduate and graduate students majoring in business and related disciplines. The library also supports the teaching and research mission of approximately 200 full-time faculty members in the areas it supports.

The Smeal College of Business Administration has approximately 6,500 undergraduate students, 200 MBA students, and several dozen Ph.D. students. The Smeal College of Business Administration offers majors in accounting, actuarial science, business logistics, finance, insurance, management and organization, management science and information systems, marketing, operations and information systems management, and real estate. In addition to the Master of Business Administration (MBA) program, Smeal College offers M.S. degrees in accounting, business logistics, finance, management science, marketing and real estate. Ph.D. programs are in the areas of accounting, business logistics, finance, insurance, management science, marketing and distribution, operations management, and real estate.

> The School of Hotel, Restaurant, and Recreation Management offers undergraduate programs in Hotel, Restaurant, and Institutional Management; Recreation and Park Management; and Professional Golf Management. Graduate programs include M.H.R.I.M., M.S., and Ph.D. programs in Hotel, Restaurant, and Institutional Management, and M.S. and Ph.D. programs in Leisure Studies. There are approximately 950 undergraduate majors and 75 graduate students in the School.

> The Department of Economics in the College of Liberal Arts offers undergraduate, master's and doctoral degrees in Economics. There are approximately 310 undergraduate economics majors and 65 graduate students. Additionally, there are over 5,000 students enrolled in economics courses each semester.

COORDINATION AND COOPERATIVE INFORMATION

The selection of materials is coordinated by the Head, Schreyer Business Library. Overlap of collections occurs most often with the Social Sciences, Engineering, and Education and Behavioral Sciences libraries. The Heads of these subject libraries work together to ensure cooperative and collaborative collection development.

> The University Libraries are members of several consortia, including the CIC (Committee for Institutional Cooperation–the Big 10) and PALCI (Pennsylvania Academic Library Consortium, Inc.). Users of the University Libraries at Penn State University have access to collections of member libraries.

SUBJECT AND LANGUAGE MODIFIERS

English language or works translated into English are preferred over non-English language materials. Emphasis is on both U.S. and international business.

DESCRIPTION OF MATERIALS COLLECTED

The Schreyer Business Library collections include all of the following formats:

Electronic & Multimedia
    Web-Based Resources*
    CD-ROM Products
    Videocassettes
    DVD
Monographs
Journals & Other Serial Publications
Conference Proceedings
Government Publications
Bibliographies
Dictionaries and Handbooks
Encyclopedias
Directories
Yearbooks
Working Papers

Textbooks are generally not collected. The Schreyer Business Library attempts to add publications of the faculty members in the units it supports. While the library does support microform collections, these are housed in the Microforms Department.

Currency is important and the Schreyer Business Library is largely concerned with materials addressing current business practices, with the exception of the history of corporations and important historical business trends or people.

The Schreyer Business Library attempts to avoid duplication of resources in multiple formats, unless they are made available for free or very inexpensively. Format decisions should be made on the basis of cost, potential use, demand, and space and other resource requirements. When other factors are equal, the electronic version is preferable due to the increased potential for a variety of uses of the information and the potential for simultaneous use.

> *The Pennsylvania State University is one university geographically dispersed, with one administrative structure and uniform programs and services. The University Libraries are also a single entity within the University. The University Libraries will therefore not partition Web-based resources by location. All Web-based resources must be made available to all Penn State users throughout the system without regard to location.

Written by Gary W. White, August 2000

APPENDIX B

THE PENNSYLVANIA STATE UNIVERSITY LIBRARIES
WOMEN'S STUDIES COLLECTION DEVELOPMENT POLICY

Fund Name and Number: WOMEN 360

Subject Specialist: Cindy Ingold, Social Sciences Librarian
                            Specialities: Women's Studies
                                             African and African American Studies
                                             Gay, Lesbian, Bisexual Studies
                            208E Paterno Library
                            865-0665 (phone)
                            863-1403 (fax)
                            cingold@psu.edu

Program Liason: Carolyn Sachs, Director, Women's Studies Program
                            101 Willard Building
                            863-4025 (phone)

I. PURPOSE AND PROGRAMMATIC INFORMATION

The women's studies collection supports the curriculum needs for the Women's Studies Program; the teaching and research needs for all faculty in all disciplines relating to women and gender; and to a lesser extent, the general and popular interests of the students and the public at large.

The Women's Studies Program at Penn State celebrated its twentieth anniversary in 1999. For several years, students could only earn an undergraduate minor in women's studies. Eventually, a graduate minor was offered, and beginning in the fall of 1991, students could earn an undergraduate major in Women's Studies from Penn State. Over the last two years, women's studies faculty have been discussing the feasibility of offering a dual-degree MA or PhD in women's studies and another field. Departments being approached to offer the dual-degree with Women's Studies include History, English, Comparative Literature, Political Science, French, and Art Education.

Many departments within the College of Liberal Arts teach women's studies courses, but other departments/programs with active faculty include nursing, family studies, art and art education. Each academic year nearly 30 courses are offered in such fields as African/African American Studies, American Studies, Anthropology, Communications, Comparative Literature, English, French, History, Human Development and Family Studies, Political

Science, Psychology, and Sociology. Women's Studies courses are offered at all Penn State locations.

Currently, there are nearly forty faculty members at the University Park campus with either budgeted or non-budgeted joint appointments. Nearly all the other locations have at least one faculty member.

II. COLLECTION DEVELOPMENT GUIDELINES

A. Subjects Covered

Purchases on the women's studies fund generally cover interdisciplinary topics that do not fit easily into a specific subject area. All works on feminist methodology and feminist theory are purchased on this fund including critiques of social, political, philosophical, and scientific theories of women and women's studies. Additionally, works from all areas of the social sciences that bring a significant feminist perspective to the topic are also purchased. Materials which might be considered popular but which deal with the status of the women's movement or current issues facing women such as *Backlash* by Susan Faludi or *Revolution from Within: A Book of Self-Esteem* by Gloria Steinem are purchased. Finally, monographs that could be considered "self-help" such as titles on eating disorders, sexual assault, or sexual harassment in the workplace are occasionally purchased as funds permit.

B. Overlap With Other Subjects/Collections

Because of the interdisciplinary nature of women's studies, there is a great deal of overlap with other subjects, funds, and departments including, but not limited to:

- African and African American Studies
- Behavioral Sciences including Family Studies, Health and Human Development, Psychology
- Comparative Literature
- Education
- Gay, Lesbian, and Bisexual Studies
- Global Studies
- Health, Nursing, Medicine
- History and Area Studies
- Labor and Industrial Relations
- All Literature funds
- Political Science
- Religious Studies
- Sociology

The amount of money allocated to the WOMEN 360 fund has increased over the last several years. However, the women's studies subject specialist works closely with other subject specialists and selectors in the University Libraries to assure that all requested materials can be purchased. In the past, large ticket items and even journal subscriptions have been purchases with monies from two or more different subject funds.

C. Languages Collected
Emphasis is placed on English language materials, with an occasional title purchased in other major European languages.

D. Geographical Limits
No region or country is excluded, but emphasis is placed on the United States and Western Europe. Within the last few years, more and more titles are being purchased about women from other areas of the world, especially Africa and Latin America.

E. Chronological Limits
Emphasis is placed on contemporary persons and topics, but material is collected relating to all time periods.

F. Types of Materials Collected and Excluded
Collected:
1. *Reference Works.* These include encyclopedias and dictionaries; directories; handbooks; and biographical works. Very few print indexes or abstracts, or print bibliographies are purchased.
2. *Academic and Trade Publications.* These include scholarly monographs; anthologies or edited works; some fiction and creative writing (most of this is purchased by the various Literature subject specialists); and some general and popular works.
3. *Small Press Titles.* Monographs from small presses, and ephemeral sources are collected on a selective basis. **NOTE:** Many monographs from academic, trade, and small presses come in through our U.S. Approval Plan with YBP. Materials are reviewed every two weeks.
4. *Periodicals.* Currently, only twenty-three periodicals are purchased on the WOMEN 360 fund. However, many other funds include periodical titles, which could be considered women's studies, or women related titles. Go to the Women's Studies home page and click on periodicals for a list of women's studies/women related periodicals. (http://www.libraries.psu.edu/crsweb/docs/women/women.htm)

5. *Government Documents.* U.S. and international documents are currently selected by subject specialists in the Social Sciences Library.
6. *Legal Materials.* The law school for The Pennsylvania State University is located at Dickinson in Carlisle, PA. However, the library collections at the University Park campus include an exceptional amount of legal materials. The Women's Studies Librarian in consultation with other librarians in Social Sciences selects many resources including monographs, reference works, and periodicals relating to feminist jurisprudence and women and the law.
7. *Special Collections.* The women's studies subject specialist does occasionally purchase special collections on microfilm. In the past five years, the PSU Libraries acquired *The Papers of Elizabeth Cady Stanton and Susan B. Anthony* on microfilm. The Penn State University Libraries also own the *History of Women* collection on microfilm, which includes titles from the Sophia Smith collection at Smith College and titles from the Schlesinger Library on the History of Women in America. This is considered the premiere collection of primary resources on women in the United States. The Libraries also owns the *Herstory* collection, which includes women's journals, newspapers, and newsletters dating from 1956 to 1974. Many other collections relating to women can be found in the Penn State Room/University Archives and in Historical Collections and Labor Archives. Finally, Penn State Harrisburg is home to the Alice Marshall Collection that includes 7,000 books and pamphlets, 400 periodicals, and thousands of other items covering over 400 years of women's history.
8. *A-V Materials.* In 1995, subject specialists and selectors from the University Libraries began purchasing videos as part of their collection development responsibilities. The women's studies specialist has added many videos to the collection in the past five years, and continues to work with faculty and students to enhance this collection.
9. *Electronic Resources.* For many years, few electronic resources other than CD-ROMs existed for women's studies. However, there are now several important electronic databases for women's studies. *Contemporary Women's Issues*, an online database of fulltext resources, was purchased in 1998, and *Women's Resources International*, an abstracting and indexing service became available in 2000. These sources are available at all Penn State locations.

Excluded:
Dissertations; textbooks; juvenile material; pamphlets; music; popular and activist periodicals and newsletters; women's newspapers.

III. OTHER CONSIDERATIONS

The women's studies specialist works closely with other library faculty and teaching faculty to assure that the most current and appropriate materials are purchased.

Several sources are consulted for collection development including *Choice*, *Library Journal*, or *Publishers Weekly*. The women's studies specialist also relies on some important women's studies collection development publications including, *The Women's Review of Books*, and three sources from the office of the Women's Studies Librarian, University of Wisconsin System: *Feminist Collections: A Quarterly of Women's Studies Resources*; *Feminist Periodicals*; and *New Books on Women & Feminism*. Suggestions from students and the general public are also taken into consideration. Finally, continuous collection assessment is important to assure that the collections are meeting the needs of all researchers, faculty, and students. This is done as time permits.

Submitted by Cindy Faries, Aug. 1996
Updated by Cindy Ingold, Feb. 2000
Reprinted with permission.

The End of an American (Library) Dream: The Rise and Decline of the Collection Development Policy Statement at Berkeley

James H. Spohrer

SUMMARY. Berkeley's Collection Development Policy Statement (CDPS) dates from 1980 and reflects the spirit of this era, written to facilitate building of comprehensive collections on the national level as well as to assist in regional cooperative efforts. Fiscal constraints (largely the result of serials inflation) have since encouraged greater emphasis on meeting immediate local needs. Despite this, the 1980 CDPS has never been systematically revised, partly due to the effort required, the impact of administrative changes (including the loss of a centralized collections office during a critical period), and uncertainty about the place of electronic resources. As the library learns to cope with inflation and to incorporate electronic resources in collection planning, a CDPS is needed to guide collection development in an age of diminished resources. Such a new CDPS must take a different approach to collection planning, providing great flexibility, allowing for long-range planning, and coordinating approaches to print and to digital collections. *[Article copies available for a fee from The Haworth Document Delivery Service: 1-800-HAWORTH. E-mail address: <docdelivery@haworthpress.com> Website: <http://www.HaworthPress.com> © 2003 by The Haworth Press, Inc. All rights reserved.]*

James H. Spohrer is Librarian for Germanic Collections, University of California, Berkeley (E-mail: jspohrer@library.berkeley.edu).

[Haworth co-indexing entry note]: "The End of an American (Library) Dream: The Rise and Decline of the Collection Development Policy Statement at Berkeley." Spohrer, James H. Co-published simultaneously in *The Acquisitions Librarian* (The Haworth Information Press, an imprint of The Haworth Press, Inc.) No. 30, 2003, pp. 33-47; and: *Collection Development Policies: New Directions for Changing Collections* (ed: Daniel C. Mack) The Haworth Information Press, an imprint of The Haworth Press, Inc., 2003, pp. 33-47. Single or multiple copies of this article are available for a fee from The Haworth Document Delivery Service [1-800-HAWORTH, 9:00 a.m. - 5:00 p.m. (EST). E-mail address: docdelivery@haworthpress.com].

http://www.haworthpress.com/store/product.asp?sku=J101
© 2003 by The Haworth Press, Inc. All rights reserved.

10.1300/J101v15n30_04

KEYWORDS. Collections, policy statements, academic libraries, University of California at Berkeley, future of collection development

Across the United States during the late 1970s and early 1980s, academic libraries began a process of codifying and regularizing their collection building practices through the creation of collection development policy statements (CDPS). The CDPS was designed to serve as a blueprint not only for local collecting and collection management policies, but also as a map for the creation of regional and national consortia[1] whose purpose was to concentrate and apply collecting resources in ways which were more clearly focussed on local needs, and at the same time to strengthen resources nationally by documenting local strengths and assigning national collecting responsibilities. Mary Bostic summarized the chief uses of the CDPS in her 1988 article *A Written Collection Development Policy*:

1. "to assign responsibility for the collecting function";
2. to "help the collection conform to the goals and objectives of the library and the university";
3. to "assist those who select materials by translating the goals and objectives into specific guidelines";
4. to assign "responsibilities of outlining relationships within a consortium or other cooperating groups of libraries"; and
5. to "serve as a means of communicating collection plans to users and administrators."[2]

As Bostic's fourth point suggests, interlibrary cooperation in collection development and management was an important factor in the decision to create a CDPS. A chief impetus for the development of the CDPS among large research libraries was the creation of the Resource Library Group's *Conspectus*, which constituted an overview arranged by subject of existing collection strengths and future collecting intensities of RLG members; it also served as the framework under which RLG member libraries, based on their local collecting needs and histories, engaged to fulfill "primary collecting responsibilities" (PCRs) for a wide variety of (often esoteric) academic disciplines and specialties. The establishment of PCRs had two purposes: first, to assure the continued strength of national holdings in these PCR fields, and secondly, to allow non-PCR institutions to rely on a single institution (or a small number of institutions) to provide collecting coverage of these subject areas, and thus to redirect their own resources to meeting more pressing local needs.

It is worth noting that the central idea of the Conspectus, "a break-down of subject fields in such as way as to allow distributed collection responsibilities for as many fields as possible,"[3] was not entirely new. In 1948 the Research Libraries Group, with support from the Carnegie Corporation, created its "Farmington Plan," a project to obtain at least one copy of "each new foreign book and pamphlet that might reasonably be expected to interest a research worker in the United States"[4] as a means of building the national stock of such materials. The Farmington Plan itself was first conceived in 1939 and grew out of U.S. librarians' (ultimately justified) fears that their access to foreign language materials would be compromised by the outbreak of hostilities in Europe, and it was chiefly in the aftermath of World War II, during European reconstruction that the Plan took shape and flourished. (As postwar reconstruction progressed on the Continent and book markets returned to a more stable and predictable state, the need for the Plan diminished in all but a few countries, and it was replaced in 1972 by the Library of Congress's so-called "PL 480" program to acquire hard-to-obtain materials from a core of developing countries.)[5]

BERKELEY'S ORIGINAL COLLECTION DEVELOPMENT POLICY STATEMENT (CDPS)

In January 1980 the Library on the Berkeley campus of the University of California published its first Collection Development Policy Statement (it was described as a "preliminary edition," and reprinted verbatim in December 1982). Its authors/editors were Dorothy Koenig, coordinator of the Collection Development Policy Project and Berkeley's Anthropology Librarian, and Sheila T. Dowd, then AUL for Collection Development and Reference Services at Berkeley.[6] It consisted of four parts:

I. *General Policies*, including a statement of the Library's missions and objectives, collections scope, subject limitations, cooperative programs, and other policies governing collection development;
II. a *Detailed Analysis by LC Class*, including a line-by-line analysis in 136 pages of the LC Classification, showing Berkeley's existing collecting levels and its collection policy level for each line;

III. an extensive list of *Appendices* including supplementary CD policy statements covering newspapers, cartographic materials, the holdings of the Bancroft (rare books and manuscripts) Library, the Undergraduate Library, East Asian language materials and Berkeley's vast reference and bibliography collections; and

IV. the *Indexes* to the classed analysis by subject and academic department.

It was an ambitious undertaking intended to serve as a point of reference for Berkeley's collecting activities in what was widely assumed to be an atmosphere of increasingly sophisticated collaboration among research libraries for collection-building purposes, in part due to the strong growth of collection size among U.S. research libraries in the thirty-five years following World War II, and also due to the new potential for collaboration which tools such as the Conspectus made possible.

In Berkeley's case, the Introduction to the CDPS cited the recent inauguration of the Stanford/Berkeley Library Cooperative Program (a cooperative document delivery project between the two Bay Area campuses created through grants from the Sloan and Mellon foundations) as a major impulsion to "draft, review, revise and disseminate a coordinated statement of collection policy for the [Berkeley] General Library."[7] The goal of the statement was to "articulate a collection policy which expresses the current needs of the Berkeley academic community." Significantly, the authors of Berkeley's CDPS added that:

> because academic programs grow and change, this policy statement must be reviewed and revised at regular intervals. Changes in specific segments may be a continuing process; a formal review of the entire policy statement, with the assistance of the Library Committee of the Academic Senate and other appropriate groups, should be conducted every five years.[8]

REASONS FOR SUBSEQUENT LACK OF REVISION

Although the Berkeley Library did begin an internal process to review and plan revisions of the CDPS in the mid-1980s, and produced a practical complement to the 1980 CDPS called the *Guide to Collection Development and Management at the University of California, Berkeley*, no systematic revision of the CDPS was ever carried out and it was never reissued in updated form. The heady optimism of the 1970s and early 1980s regarding collection growth and expanding opportunities for collaborative collection-building were replaced as that decade approached its end by a growing fear that the costs of building deep, rich academic library resources were outstripping their institutions' ability to afford them, and by a growing realization that in a climate of deteriorating collection budgets, the attractiveness of consortial collecting diminished as institutions focused their shrinking fiscal resources increasingly on local needs for heavily-used material. The rationale for institutions' acceptance of "primary collecting responsibility" within RLG and other cooperative structures also waned, as individual libraries found themselves faced in the late eighties and the first half of the 1990s with wave after wave of serials cancellations; this made the maintenance of active local collection-building efforts for esoteric subjects to meet national needs much more difficult to justify, even in relatively well-financed institutions such as Berkeley's library. In addition, collection development specialists found themselves forced by circumstances to redirect collection resources away from less frequently used items such as foreign language materials and special subjects (even those for which they had long and prolific collecting histories), and toward the serial and monographic publications in highest demand among their clientele. Moreover, as the 1990s progressed, a third factor entered the picture to further cloud the fiscal picture for library collections: the steady growth of an array of electronic resources, ranging from sophisticated bibliographic citation retrieval tools to vast raw data sets, required collection development librarians to question their basic historical assumptions about allocation of CD budgets and programmatic growth of print collections. Estimates of the future impact of digital materials on traditional print collection ranged from the assumption in some quarters that it would be decades before any meaningful academic digital content came into general use, to the conviction that digital resources would completely dominate the market for scholarly research materials within a few short years. In that climate of extremes, rational planning for the effects of digital resources on the collection development mix at any given institution was essentially futile.

At Berkeley, all these factors combined to create a situation in which no regular revisions of the 1980 "preliminary" CDPS has ever taken place, and moreover one in which it now appears unlikely under current circumstances that the goal of regular revisions of the Library's CDPS will ever be achieved. Already in the late 1980s, as the creeping growth in cost of serials subscriptions began to signal first a reduction and then a catastrophic failure of the Library's ability to maintain the quality and scope of both its serials collections and its monographs acquisitions, the CDPS was increasingly regarded as an irrelevance, particularly in the face of the need to restructure collections fundamentally through serials cancellations, elimination of virtually all serial *and* monographic duplication, radical de-emphasis on building the undergraduate collections,[9] and a move away from acquisition of less-used materials.[10] The great sweep of subject categories covered in the 1980 CDPS was seen as an unaffordable luxury for a CD budget under siege, and with the passage of time, the "level of existing collections" and "collecting policy level" for each one began progressively to lend the whole document a strangely fictional quality in the light of 1990s collecting practices. Plus, the enormous physical labor required for CDPS revision seemed to be far beyond the Library's ability to undertake, it having lost without replacement 37% of its professional librarians due to a combination of normal attrition and incentives for early retirement between 1989 and 1999.

FACTORS ENCOURAGING A NEW CDPS

As Berkeley's collection budgets were gradually rebuilt during the late 1990s, and as the positive fiscal impact of the California Digital Library in building electronic collections began to be felt at the local campus level, a sense of at least temporary relief from the devastating fiscal pressures of the last decade has arisen. In this context, three factors have converged to make revisitation of the Berkeley CDPS a prudent planning strategy, at least in principle:

> *first*, the renewed campus commitment to maintain deep, strong print collections in areas of interest to Berkeley researchers;

> *secondly*, the emergence of an effective UC-wide consortial approach to the question of digital acquisitions (at least those in English), which removes much of the uncertainly about funding these materials from local calculations;

> and *finally*, a sense that some alternative strategies for journal pricing have begun to emerge, giving us reason to hope that realistic program-based ratios for serials and monographs can once again form the basis for sound, pragmatic long-term collection growth planning.

In addition, the chronic understaffing of collection development (and many other operational areas) at Berkeley has slowly begun to be addressed, and there is reason to hope that its corps of selectors will again reach a level of at least nominal adequacy. Nonetheless more than twenty years have elapsed since the first groundbreaking work in analyzing and describing the Berkeley collections, and it is fair to say that the 1980 CDPS can now no longer serve as a valid starting point in formulating Berkeley's current collecting policies.

It is interesting to observe the effect of the fiscal perturbations on Berkeley's collecting effort in the years since the 1980 CDPS was issued. In gross ARL statistical terms, the Library's current serials subscriptions declined by over 22% between their 1980 level and that of 1999, gross volumes added dropped from the 1985 all-time high of 301,000 volumes to the 1999 level of 166,459 volumes, and total items borrowed through ILB increased by over 130% from 9,988 items in 1980 to over 23,000 in 1999.[11] While many factors in addition to the fiscal ones mentioned here have contributed to these changes, there is no doubt that this twenty-year period has seen a radical reorientation of Berkeley's collecting policies and practices. Without even factoring in the irretrievable material losses of the 1990s, it is fair to say that, despite the progress made since 1998, the Library's current collecting levels for print publications remain substantially below those of the 1980s.

By the same token, Berkeley's participation in cooperative collecting activities has also been affected by the fiscal pressures which constrained it during this period. While the Berkeley and Stanford libraries did extend their bilateral collection development and document delivery collaboration to include the University of Texas-Austin for Latin American materials in 1997, Berkeley's own participation in RLG cooperative ventures has dwindled to virtually nothing. And even its support for such national cooperative projects as CRL's foreign microfilm projects and the Library of Congress's array of overseas acquisitions programs has been repeatedly called into question and/or progressively compromised over the years. Berkeley's CDPS, once intended as the equivalent of at least a local map to the policy of contributing to national collection development priorities, is as outdated as a real city map of Berkeley in 1980 would be for a traveler of today.

CONSTRAINTS HINDERING REVISION OF THE CDPS

What occurred during the twenty years following the publication of the 1980 "preliminary" edition of the Berkeley CDPS and the present day to move research libraries away from their emphasis on the creation of these ambitious planning documents? There were a number of factors on the national and local scenes which exploded the idealized paradigm underlying the Conspectus and the CDPS. One was undoubtedly that the amount of effort and expertise required to create a CDPS for a large research institution proved so monumental that, once finished with the basic ("preliminary") policy statement, institutions such as Berkeley simply could not muster the collective energy to duplicate and extend that effort in revising it. While collection development staffing at Berkeley remained relatively stable through most of the 1980s, near the end of that decade and all through the 1990s the loss of both selector expertise and administrative continuity led to a climate in which the Library lacked the margin of FTE necessary to undertake CDPS revision.

Another contributing factor to the failure to act on CDPS revision was the combined effect of California's economic recession in the first half of the 1990s which, coupled with runaway inflation in academic journal prices in scientific, technical and medical fields, sowed chaos in the year-to-year budget planning for collections during that period. The Library at Berkeley found the basic economic premises underlying its original CDPS (and the vision of national cooperation which it implied) eroded to the point of irrelevance due to the cumulative effects of these events. Berkeley and other UC campuses (indeed ultimately U.S. research libraries as a whole) were required to make deep cuts in serials expenditures in order to offset the consequences of price inflation for materials (chiefly serials), and this had the double effect of forcing them to channel scarce collecting resources increasingly into mainstream materials and away from rarely-held items, and negating their attractiveness as potential cooperative partners.

This situation was exacerbated at Berkeley by a period of administrative turmoil which began with the retirement of University Librarian Joseph Rosenthal in 1991; in the period 1991-2000 that position was held by a total of six individuals, variously having temporary and permanent appointments for terms which averaged only 20 months each. In such an environment of constant leadership change, and particularly in the light of the administrative reorganization which each change usually produced, many important policy issues, including those dealing with Berkeley's collection development policy, were necessarily put off in the expectation of a more stable future climate for decision-making.

IMPACT OF INFLATION ON LIBRARY COOPERATION

There was a third factor which also influenced the Library's willingness and ability to take up the global question of collections policy in the form of a revision of the CDPS. A subtle change in the campus position regarding cooperative collecting emerged during the course of the financial crisis playing itself out in the UC system at that time. This change played an important role in determining the University's support for collection development, and by implication its interest in the evolution of its CD policy, especially insofar as it concerned cooperative collecting practices. The Berkeley campus administration had long supported Library initiatives to increase interlibrary collection development cooperation, primarily with other UC campus libraries and with its "special" partner Stanford,[12] but also in the context of larger national consortia such as RLG and CRL. Nonetheless it emerged as an outgrowth of the economic difficulties which the University faced in the early 1990s that the campus administration began to view the process of collaborative collection development as chiefly a means of "economization" (in the strict sense of reduction of CD expenditures), as a way out of the economic crisis facing the Library's acquisition programs.

This ultimately took the form of a stance on the part of Berkeley's campus administration that it would no longer automatically support the costs of library materials inflation, and in particular what it considered the exorbitant cost of journal inflation. Cooperation for mutual enrichment of resources was transformed into cooperation as a means of relying on other institutions to meet a part of the basic collection needs of Berkeley scholars. New funding for cooperation, in the form of supplemental allocations to encourage collaboration, disappeared from the Library's collection budget, and even traditional intercampus methods of joint financing of major purchases were eliminated as the campus concentrated its depleted resources exclusively on its narrow local mission. As a consequence of that position, virtually all collection development planning in the Library shifted to a footing of damage control (both in the fiscal sense of maintaining budgetary discipline and in the sense of good library stewardship by limiting the permanent damage to the collections), in which serials subscriptions were repeatedly reduced, duplication of high-use materials was virtually eliminated among the various components of the Library system, and the average annual rate of monographic acquisitions plummeted.[13]

UNIVERSITY OF CALIFORNIA, BERKELEY
VOLUMES ADDED, GROSS

1980	169,922	1990	202,202
1981	184,540	1991	188,270
1982	209,264	1992	176,620
1983	230,171	1993	144,157
1984	241,688	1994	156,040
1985	301,411	1995	155,586
1986	254,231	1996	173,149
1987	206,181	1997	167,378
1988	195,012	1998	155,007
1989	195,076	1999	166,459

IMPACT OF LOSS OF CENTRALIZED PLANNING OFFICE

One more important factor contributed to the sense of rudderlessness in collecting matters when the Library's financial retrenchment was at its apogee: in 1996 the Library once again reorganized its administrative structure, eliminating the position of AUL for Collections and dividing collections management responsibility among three "subject" AULs, for Science and Technology, for Social Sciences and for Humanities and Area Studies. While there were some logical reasons for the new structure (in particular it allowed the Library to align itself more closely with campus academic structures), it resulted in a lack of concentrated authority for global collections issues. Collection development policy questions became the province of a committee, itself largely aligned on subject axes, which tended to lack the critical distance necessary to deal with broad general questions spanning numerous disciplines. As a result, during the period 1996-1999, no single Library administrator was the "official" spokesman for collections, and the result was a lack of clarity and forcefulness in communicating collections issues (in particular the urgency of the economic situation) to both the campus and to Library staff as a whole.

This in turn led to a presumption on the part of campus administrators that the Library had no real plan for long-term development of collections, and in the absence of a viable, current CDPS the Library had little to offer in rebuttal of that presumption. Since, moreover, the campus had placed great hope in the belief that digital technology would quickly lead to a sharp reduction in the need for funds to purchase traditional print materials, the result was a kind of "revolution of rising expectations" among these administrators. Confident that new technology was making the printed book obsolete at a rapid rate, and convinced that the Library had no reliable ability to predict future collections needs (or at least that it did not speak with one voice on these questions), campus administrators ultimately chose not to believe the Library's dire claims about the seriousness of the collections resources situation. Out of this impasse there arose at some point a fatal conviction among many in the Library administration that it was useless to even argue the case for increased collections resources, and that instead the Library should simply acquiesce in what was apparently the campus's desire to see the collections significantly reduced.

Although arguments have been made to the effect that reductions in the rate of general collections resource growth unfairly penalized fields such as the humanities and social sciences (where journal cost inflation was much more modest on the whole), there is no doubt that the carnage in the Library's collecting program was general; no subject grouping or geographic area was spared, and enormous expenditures of time and effort on the part of the Library's collection development staff were required on a nearly annual basis to devise methods to share the burden of the cuts equitably and to carry them out in a responsible manner. There is an irony in the fact that so much Library staff effort went into planning and implementing the program to reduce the collections at exactly the moment when staff were in shortest supply and the need for competent collection policy planning was at its apex.

It also suggests that the original conceptual framework for the Berkeley CDPS as a predictive tool was hopelessly optimistic and inadequate, based as it was upon a flawed set of financial assumptions ultimately overturned by the combination of changes in the economics of scholarly publishing and a serious, prolonged downturn in the state's economy. To restore credibility to the predictive quality of the CDPS, any future iterations of it must take into account the eventuality, and perhaps the inevitability, of such changes in the fiscal and commercial environment.

LESSONS LEARNED: A NEW VIEW OF CDPS NEEDS

What are the lessons which Berkeley has learned from the past twenty years in terms of collection planning and the real obstacles to creating and maintaining a utilitarian collection development policy statement of reasonable currency and flexibility? The first one which comes to mind is that as an institution, the university and the Library must commit jointly and firmly to the effort required not only to create the statement but also to maintain it at a level of accuracy and timeliness which will insure that it serves some useful purpose over time. The CDPS may take the apparent form of a snapshot of current collecting practices, but the real measure of its usefulness is to allow libraries to inject elements of volitional institutional direction into what otherwise inevitably becomes a process by which the library materials budget feeds on its own momentum and grows in the direction which that momentum imparts. For indeed, although the CDPS is chiefly viewed as a document to shape Library planning with regard to collections, the broader campus administration as both the ultimate source of funding for collections and the arbiter of institutional goals and priorities, should play an integral role in the shaping, implementation and evaluation over time of the CDPS. It is after all a key planning document for the single largest category of expenditures in one of the university's chief concentrations of fiscal and programmatic assets, and the success of the collection-building effort is the single most important issue in the Library's fulfillment of its overall mission. It is too important an issue to be left entirely to the discretion of a library administration, and in a climate of administrative turbulence such as the one Berkeley experienced in the 1990s, it is easy to see the consequences of such neglect.

A second conclusion, in the event that the Library attempts at some future point to create and maintain a planning structure similar to the 1980 CDPS, is that the economic assumptions which underlie such a document must be the subject of serious reflection in advance of its establishment. A concomitant is that the university would do well to consider providing the Library with rolling multi-year commitments in advance for its collection funding, in order to prevent the necessity for making changes (with either positive or negative consequences) in collection policy on very short notice. In fact, the events of the past two decades have underscored the importance of the CDPS as a campus and a library planning tool, with the corresponding implication that some provision for reliability and continuity of data (in the form of two- or three-year advance commitments of campus resources) must be present. Given the daunting logistics of both gearing up and gearing down the Library's acquisitions program, it is prudent to replace year-to-year global funding decisions—which sometimes leave only a few months for library staff to carry out required changes—with a reliable planning window of longer duration. Taking such a long view would also allow both the Library and the university to better plan for the staffing consequences of directional shifts in library collection development policies.

A final conclusion also suggests itself: given the growth of digital collections, and the emergence of effective cooperative structures such as the California Digital Library to manage at least the most commonly-used electronic resources, the Library must develop a parallel planning track to describe and monitor the digital collections themselves. Moreover, since there is increasingly an intersection of user expectations and user benefits between digital and print resources, the policy statement for the development of print collections needs to be continually compared to that for digital collections to insure that the two types of collections are developed in rational and mutually enhancing ways.

CONCLUSIONS:
ARGUMENTS FOR A COMPREHENSIVE CDPS

What advantages could the Library and the University expect to derive from a renewed commitment to a collection development policy statement?[14] First of all, it would provide the institution with a powerful tool for budget planning, allowing it to predict more faithfully the true costs of redirection in campus teaching and research programs, and to build into such planning timeframes the duration necessary to achieve a specific goal of redirection. Secondly, it can serve as the normative point of insertion of both faculty and campus administrative concerns into Library planning models, allowing timely modification of those planning models in a manner which would ultimately enhance rather than disrupt instructional and research programs which depend on the Library. No university administration can afford to be ignorant of the rationales, methods, goals and results of its library's collection development program, and the involvement of the campus administration in the conception and execution of the CDPS is a good means of insuring seamless communication on these crucial issues. Third, a thorough and up-to-date CDPS gives the Library's collection program credibility both among its local clientele and among potential institutional partners in cooperative collection development and document delivery programs. The absence of a planning structure such as the CDPS is a clear indication to potential partners that a given institution does not have a consistent, integral long-range approach to its own collection-building needs, and that it may prove an unreliable partner over time in the elaboration of mutually-beneficial cooperative structures. In simple terms, the CDPS is the embodiment of a kind of social contract between the library and its clienteles, both local and extramural, and like all such contracts, its currency is an essential feature of its validity.

In summary, the auspicious start in 1980 of Berkeley's Collection Development Policy Statement, and its gradual abandonment as the circumstantial facts upon which it was based became obsolete, are a testament to the notion that collections planning must be viewed as an ongoing, organic activity which is as crucial to overall institutional health as any other aspect of library operations. It is disappointing to reflect that the great efforts required to create the 1980 CDPS amount now to nothing more than a historical footnote, since the planning momentum which it embodied has now been replaced by an equally impressive institutional inertia on the subject. We must once again realize that planning for collection development cannot be an occasional or optional activity for research libraries, or one which is pursued only in response to either emergencies or fashions in library management; it must be a fully integrated part of our overview of a library's institutional health and prospects for the future. Just as we must constantly scan the horizon for new models of staffing, new technological advances for both clientele and staff, and new means of dealing with the problems of spatiality which are the inevitable result of library growth over time, so too must we begin again to view collections growth and evolution as key elements in our preparations to meet the academic challenges of the future.

NOTES

1. Charles Willett's article "International Collaboration among Acquisitions Librarians" (*IFLA Journal,* vol. 11 (4) 1985, 289-296), even put forward a persuasive case for transnational cooperation among libraries in building international resources, basing his optimism on the success of such groups as the Seminar on the Acquisition of Latin American Library Materials (SALALM). Regrettably, not much has been systematically accomplished in this regard in the intervening years, although the Research Libraries Group has sponsored "demonstration projects" involving international cooperation in providing access to Japanese, Latin American and German materials.

2. *Collection Management,* vol. 10 (3/4), (1988), 91-92.

3. Research Libraries Group, Inc. "Summary Minutes of the Meeting of the Collection Development and Management Committee," (New Haven, CT: Yale University Press, 1989), 2. Quoted from Bostic (1988), 98. See also the remarkable summary of the Conspectus project by Nancy Gwinn and Paul Mosher, "Coordinating Collection Development: the RLG Conspectus" *College & Research Libraries,* vol. 44 (2), 1983, 128-140.

4. Edwin E. Williams, *Farmington Plan Handbook* (Bloomington: Association of Research Libraries, 1953), 3.

5. David H. Stam ("Think Globally, Act Locally: Collection Development and Resource Sharing," *Collection Building,* vol. 5 (1) Spring 1983, 20) writes of the "failure of the Farmington Plan," but it is equally possible to see its demise as a natural one caused by the shifting market forces discussed above. It had outlived its usefulness in large part, and the residual need was met by a new program–P.L. 480–which more closely corresponded to the circumstances then in vigor.

6. For an excellent overview of the entire project at Berkeley, see Dorothy Koenig's article "Rushmore at Berkeley: the Dynamics of Developing a Written Collection Development Policy Statement," *The Journal of Academic Librarianship,* vol. 7 (6), January 1982, 344-350.

7. *Collection Development Policy Statement* (Berkeley: General Library, University of California, Berkeley, 1980, page 1.

8. Ibid., p. 2. This insistence on periodic revision was a part of the regular CDPS mantra of the period. See, e.g., Scott R. Bullard, "Collection Management and Development Institute, Stanford University, July 6-10, 1981, the LAPT Report, *Library Acquisitions: Practice and Theory,* vol. 5 (3/4) 1981, 179, 182.

9. At Berkeley this is still a discrete entity, albeit severely weakened vis-à-vis its original conception.

10. The operative slogan, in imitation of a then-popular notion of Japanese manufacturing techniques, was "just in time" acquisition (meaning via fast interlibrary borrowing) rather than "just in case" acquisition (referring to the presumably nefarious practice of acquiring materials because of their intrinsic worth and not because of an assumption they would receive frequent use).

11. All these figures have been generated by consulting the ARL interactive statistical website at http://fisher.lib.Virginia.EDU/newarl/.

12. Chiefly through a program in the 1970s and 1980s called variously the "Major Purchase Program" and the "UC/Stanford Cooperative Collections Plan," an annual meeting of UC and Stanford collection development heads to discuss and act on lists of expensive purchases which were financed and held in common by the institutions in question, with specially expedited interlibrary lending provisions for participants. The program was briefly, partially and modestly resuscitated in the early 1990s, but then definitively abandoned at the height of the financial crisis.

13. According to the ARL Statistics, Berkeley's average annual monographic acquisitions rate in the ten-year period from 1980-1989 was 218,750 volumes per year, while the average annual rate for 1990-1999 was 168,487 volumes, an average annual reduction of 50,263 volumes per year, or a drop of 22.9% from the previous decade.

14. It is only fair to note that there are many who would dispute the value of a return to collection development by policy statement. See for example Dan C. Hazen's article "Collection Development Policies in the Information Age," *College & Research Libraries,* vol. 56, January 1995, 29-31. This genial screed against the current relevance of the CDPS is nonetheless tempered by the author's closing suggestion to develop format-blind descriptions of collecting practice–an intelligent and progressive variation on the theme. He does not, however, address the potential value of the CDPS as a predictive tool in collection development planning.

Using a Collection Development Curriculum as a Model for Developing Policy Documents in Practice

Sheila S. Intner

SUMMARY. This article describes the term project developed by students in the author's course in Collection Development and Management at Simmons College's Graduate School of Library and Information Science, which covers much more than the traditional "selection" guidelines. It suggests how course assignments covering components of the project might serve as a model for policy development in libraries and other information agencies. It also amplifies the model by discussing ways in which a real world policy development project differs from the academic model, and offers recommendations about how selected elements might be expanded, altered, and implemented. Particular attention is given to collection evaluation, which the author has often been asked to do or assist libraries in doing in her extracurricular work as a library consultant. *[Article copies available for a fee from The Haworth Document Delivery Service: 1-800-HAWORTH. E-mail address: <docdelivery@haworthpress.com> Website: <http://www.HaworthPress.com> © 2003 by The Haworth Press, Inc. All rights reserved.]*

Sheila S. Intner is Professor, Graduate School of Library & Information Science, Simmons College, and Director, GSLIS in Western Massachusetts, Mt. Holyoke College.

Address correspondence to Sheila S. Intner at: 11 Hupi Woods Circle; P.O. Box 151, Monterey, MA 01245-0151 (E-mail: sheila.intner@simmons.edu or shemat@aol.com).

[Haworth co-indexing entry note]: "Using a Collection Development Curriculum as a Model for Developing Policy Documents in Practice." Intner, Sheila S. Co-published simultaneously in *The Acquisitions Librarian* (The Haworth Information Press, an imprint of The Haworth Press, Inc.) No. 30, 2003, pp. 49-62; and: *Collection Development Policies: New Directions for Changing Collections* (ed: Daniel C. Mack) The Haworth Information Press, an imprint of The Haworth Press, Inc., 2003, pp. 49-62. Single or multiple copies of this article are available for a fee from The Haworth Document Delivery Service [1-800-HAWORTH, 9:00 a.m. - 5:00 p.m. (EST). E-mail address: docdelivery@haworthpress.com].

http://www.haworthpress.com/store/product.asp?sku=J101
© 2003 by The Haworth Press, Inc. All rights reserved.
10.1300/J101v15n30_05

KEYWORDS. Collection development, curriculum, policy models, practical applications

THEORY AND PRACTICE IN COLLECTION DEVELOPMENT

The perennial tug-of-war between the work done by students for their academic courses, usually perceived as theoretical or quasi-theoretical in nature, and the work that librarians and information specialists do in the real world of practice is well known. The contrast between theory and practice or these two types of work-when-done-for-educational-purposes is likely to have persisted since the beginning of library education. Nearly every book or paper dealing with the subject of professional education for library and information service mentions it, and some devote considerable space to it.[1]

Some observers divide the broad range of educational experiences associated with conveying professional knowledge into two categories–that which one learns in a formal degree-earning program and everything else–linking the former to theory and the latter to practice. Although neat and attractive in its simplicity, this classification does not hold up very well. By its definitions, if a supervisor gives a reference desk employee one-on-one instruction in searching a database, it is practical training; but if a professor or library science librarian gives that same lesson to a student in a library/information science course with an assignment to retrieve something from the database, it is theoretical education. The range of experiences that educate, academically, and train, practically, are too diverse to categorize so casually or easily.

Over the years, curricula in university-based degree-granting programs in library and information science have evolved from imparting primarily practical skills (such as learning to write catalog cards with "library hand") to developing what can rightfully be called a knowledge base,[2] and the degrees themselves have expanded from pre-baccalaureate certificates and/or baccalaureates to advanced degrees at the master's and doctoral levels.[3] Similarly, the scope of the professional knowledge base has expanded by adding a group of multidisciplinary fields to the familiar subject areas of cataloging, classification, bibliography, reference, scholarship, and publishing, which include information science, management, computing and technology, communications, teaching, and other fields. As a result, however, it is increasingly difficult to fit everything a new professional needs to know for a job into the typical master's degree program schedule.

Different strategies have been employed over the years to inject some experiential learning into formal educational programs in order to achieve a more equitable balance between theory (learning about doing something) and practice (doing it), such as offering credit for hours spent working in internships or practica, though these are not the only methods. Negotiating educationally viable internships and practica is no easy task, creating hours of work for both faculty advisers and information agency supervisors. The supervisors, in particular, must agree to invest their time working with students who are certain to leave almost immediately upon reaching the point at which they have learned enough to be valuable to the agency. In 1994, however, Elizabeth Futas examined internships and practica in relation to collection development and concluded they were not as effective in teaching skills used for collection development as they might be for other subjects, though this could change.[4] Futas said, "Therefore, the practicum experience in the area of collection development is perhaps not often the best use of the student's, field supervisor's, or faculty supervisor's time and energy. . . . As technology plays a more important role in the area of collection development and as more library and information agencies become interested in writing collection policy documents, students can play a successful role through practicums. Until that time, this analysis suggests that collection development practicums should focus on areas in which student contributions can be made within the timeframe available and should exclude those areas in which it is not possible to provide a meaningful experience in the context of a library school course."[5]

This author believes firmly that professional education needs to be grounded in practice even though it may take place within the protected environment of academia. She has tried to make students' coursework simulate the world of practice as closely as it can. Several of her syllabi, including the one for collection development, introduce the course by suggesting the student imagine himself or herself as the newly appointed officer in charge of the specified area for a real library (or information center, learning center, school library media center, or archives) with assignments that emulate the kinds of tasks real collection development officers are expected to do (see Appendix A, p. 58). For twenty years, this crossover from practice to the classroom seems to have succeeded in teaching useful skills in an academic setting. Recently, however, she has begun to believe that a reverse crossover from theory to practice is equally viable, and that the classroom exercises could have potential value to practitioners. This idea is explored in the following section.

LIS 453:
A CASE STUDY OF COLLECTION
DEVELOPMENT CURRICULUM

LIS 453, titled "Collection Development and Management," is a semester-long, four-credit elective course in the Simmons College Graduate School of Library and Information Science master's degree curriculum.[6] The author has been teaching the course at least once a year since 1988, after having first taught similar material as an Adjunct Associate Professor at Pratt Institute several years earlier. The educational product (or, in more familiar parlance, "term project") of the course, which each student must prepare, is a fully-developed, stand-alone policy-and-procedures manual for a real information agency that could be used as a strategic plan for collecting. "Fully-developed" is defined as containing an introduction to the agency's parent body and the agency's own environment, a needs assessment based on the people being served and their collection-related activities; collecting goals and objectives to meet the identified needs; an evaluation of existing collections; selection and deselection guidelines, including appropriate intellectual freedom, preservation, and cooperative program policy statements; a bibliography of selection tools; and a budget that supports the collecting plan. Other materials may also be included, according to each student's ideas about how to make this a useful tool for the agency's collecting program. Some of this material (the goals and objectives and the budget) is expected to change in each subsequent collecting cycle (most often a year), but much of it (parent body description, selection and deselection guidelines) could remain valuable for a great deal longer than that.

The term project is analyzed into eight components, each of which is a separate written assignment (see Appendix A, pp. 59-61). Students hand in these assignments twice: once as a draft at a designated class session a week or more after the professor has covered the material; and once as part of the completed project. The drafts are not graded. Instead, the professor provides comments and suggestions for needed improvement, and an indication of the grade the work would have received had it been a graded assignment. That way, students are not penalized for making mistakes, omitting needed detail, or, in some cases, missing the point of the assignment altogether. They have time to revise their work in response to the comments and suggestions (and are aware of what grade the work will earn if they do not respond), and earn a higher grade on the finished document, which constitutes the lion's share of their final grade for the course.

In a 13-week semester, the assignments are carefully timed so that six are each allotted one week, while two–the evaluation and the budget–each have two weeks. A tenth, final assignment is combining all the foregoing into a seamless, integrated document, which must be completed and handed in at the penultimate class. At the last class session, the author hands back all the term projects with written comments and grades. In a 14-week semester,[7] there is some respite with an additional week available for assembling the final document.

The topic for the last class usually is "Collection Development Career Paths," for which the author prepares a review of relevant job postings for the previous two or three years and discusses different factors that ought to be considered in taking entry-level jobs if one is aiming, eventually, to be the collection development officer for an information agency. This serious material occupies more or less time of the last class, depending on the group's desire to give themselves a farewell party. (In fact, nearly all the students have done so much work, kept to the back-breaking schedule so scrupulously, and produced such amazingly good projects, the author believes they are entitled to celebrate. Whether or not a party materializes, however, seems to depend on the number of graduating students in the group–the more graduates, the more likely a party will happen.)

HOW THE ACADEMIC EXERCISE COULD BE USED IN PRACTICE

A library that wanted to create a collection development policy could take the structure of the model policy from LIS 453 and use it as a skeleton for its own document, as well as a kind of methodology for the policy development process. The eight assignments constituting the bulk of the term project mirror elements that ought to appear as sections in any library's collection development policy and procedures manual: (1) an introduction to the parent organization–a college or university; corporation; school or school district; or a city, town, or other community–describing its mission, goals and objectives, special concerns, overall resources, environment, activities, and the people the library serves; (2) an overview of the library itself, including its history, environment, resources, traditions, standard operations, and special concerns; (3) the goals and objectives for collecting materials in the next operating cycle, based on the "needs analysis" implicit or, preferably, explicitly laid out in the foregoing descriptions; (4) a profile of the collection; (5) an evaluation of collection quality; (6) a list of collecting tools; (7) a budget for the collecting cycle; and (8) guidelines for selecting new materials and deselecting existing materials in all formats, which often includes intellectual freedom statements, policies on gifts, and obligations to cooperative partnerships, etc. While these are often augmented by other things, some merely stylistic (title pages, tables of contents, etc.) and some substantive (declarations of authority for decisions and approvals, validation of intellectual freedom policies, etc.), they are likely to occupy the lion's share of the whole document.

Each of the eight elements could constitute a portion of the development process. Collection development officers and others responsible for documenting policies and procedures could use each element as an umbrella topic, hold meetings with all the players in the institution or community to establish the contents of that element, make decisions, create and revise draft statements, and, after consultation with all the players, write the final version. The development process sounds and is lengthy and cumbersome, but if one tries to proceed more efficiently by eliminating all the meetings, consultation, and revision, one is likely to find the players are unwilling to subscribe to the results.

ACCOMMODATIONS TO THE REAL WORLD

Having the structure, however, is only the first step. The real work of creating an effective document lies in negotiating consensus on the content of each part of the policy. In practice, it is not always easy to achieve broad consensus on anything, even the factual elements such as the descriptions of the library and its parent institution or community, let alone on any of the more sensitive and controversy-provoking elements, such as goals and objectives, priorities, budget allocations, selection guidelines, etc. The best procedure is to take the time needed to involve as many institutional and community groups as possible in the effort, and resolve as many issues as possible by informing and persuading these players. As already mentioned, when each element is drafted, concerns need to be expressed and addressed, subjected to more study, or agreed to for a limited time after which the results are to be reviewed.

Collecting policies–like all policies–have political and economic ramifications that affect both the balance of power and its locus within the institution. People tend to jump on changes with alacrity, particularly if they involve money. "How dare you downsize my budget when you have increased X's!" is an expected response if a department's allocation is decreased (can we call it deallocating?), and you can be certain some individuals in each department will track every penny it is allocated. If money was no object, all allocations could be increased–some more than others to achieve shifts in collection emphasis. But in recent years, few institutions and communities have had the wherewithal to increase selected areas without taking money away from others believed to be needed less often or by fewer people. Shaping collections differently than the past to meet changing times and needs means making the hard choices to take away as well as to bestow. Compromises must also be made, often, when political muscle succeeds in retaining money that might be better used in areas demonstrating more intense need. That is one reason the collecting policy should begin with a thorough, carefully-drawn needs analysis, so any reader can see, clearly, where more materials are critical for service and where they are not.

One of the more difficult problems, both for students and practitioners, is to relate the needs of the library's public to viable collection goals and objectives. One wants to set goals and objectives that are ambitious, but reachable; capable of producing tangible benefits to the institution or community; and, within a reasonable period of time, recognizably different to collection users. It is less of a problem, though still a tricky matter, to translate the collection goals and objectives into a financial plan that succeeds in implementing them. As a reader moves through the manual, the flow of informed action should be clear, namely, that the goals and objectives derive from people's information needs and that fulfillment of those needs is consistent with institutional or community mission and goals.

Looking at stylistic matters, a real-world manual needs several elements that aren't covered in the eight components described above. The manual itself needs an introduction giving a rationale for its existence, a very brief description of its contents, and acknowledgements to those who prepared it. Explanations of how the document is to be used in practice should also be made at the outset as well as the duration its policies are expected to be in force and methods for amending and updating it. Given the likely length of the document–25 pages or more–it would benefit from having a table of contents, a list of tables, charts, and other illustrations, and an index. A title page containing basic bibliographic data would be welcomed by catalogers, while section or chapter title pages might make it easier to use. A bibliography of the sources consulted in its preparation should be included at the end of each section or at the end of the document, as preferred, but in no case should they be absent. Summaries of complex sections are useful for non-library readers, and an executive summary for the whole text should be provided as well.

The order of the elements can be shifted. Nearly everyone is likely to put the introductory sections at the beginning of the manual, but they might be followed by the collection profile and evaluation, which reveals where the collection stands at the moment. Having introduced the institution, the public, and their activities, and established the collection's status quo, it seems appropriate to move next to the goals and objectives for the cycle–where the collection should go–followed by the budget, since it is the financial plan for implementing the goals and objectives. These elements set the path for the collection as a whole, and most certainly should precede statements about how to select (and deselect) individual items or which tools to consult in selecting them.

Many large research libraries have chosen to use the conspectus framework as their guide for setting collection goals and objectives.[8] Collection developers say they will collect at the "research" or "study" level, or level "3E," or whatever. Conspectus levels provide a convenient shorthand, but as goals and objectives they are inherently problematic, since they take no account of information production during the cycle and, thus, throw cost control to the winds. The conspectus makes possible meaningful comparisons among collections by providing standardized breakdowns of subjects and ways of defining collection contents, but since no one can predict how many publications will appear in the next collecting cycle, and what forms they will take (books, articles, databases, websites, videos, etc.), one cannot know how much money will be needed to achieve the specified levels. (When students go from the needs analysis directly to expressions of desired conspectus levels, they are directed to translate them into budget allocations, which makes them rethink conspectus as a means of expressing goals and objectives.)

When all the elements have been covered, which could take as long as a year or more, the collection development manual is complete, or nearly so, with the addition of whatever useful finding aids, summaries, and specifications an individual library wishes to add to it. Once done, it should be easier to keep up to date–not only the elements that obviously need to be revised annually (or with each collecting cycle, if it is not annually), but also the elements that change more slowly, such as the library and institutional or community environment, current interpretations of institutional missions, etc. Moreoover, baseline data will have been established for collection profiles and quality evaluations, thus facilitating their continuous updating. (Some librarians are surprised to discover that all the work of evaluating a collection needs to be redone as often as is feasible–preferably once a collecting cycle.)

CONCLUSIONS

For twenty years, this author has tried taking the activities of practice and incorporating them into her classes, giving students experience in doing work they might have to do in the future in their library jobs. Now, in the particular matter of creating collection development manuals, it seems that librarians could benefit from taking the activities of students in a formal library/information science school course and incorporating them into practice. Can they succeed? Hundreds of student projects ranging in size from 35 or 40 to 150 pages in length attest to the viability of producing comprehensive manuals using the process described above. Some of the best of the projects have earned their authors professional jobs upon graduation and/or have been adopted "for real" by the libraries on which they were based. Others have merely earned their authors a good grade and credit for the course.

In a way, the LIS 453 term project does for collection development policy making what the conspectus does for evaluation: it specifies how to break down a huge undertaking into manageable chunks, and suggests what the contents of each chunk should be. Given this skeleton and blueprint for fleshing it out, librarians could be well on their way to having practical, useful, comprehensive collection development manuals.

ENDNOTES

1. Two books devoted entirely to the issue are *Theorie et pratique dans l'enseignement des sciences de l'information = Bridging the Gap between Theory and Practice*, Rejean Savard, ed. (Montreal: University of Montreal, 1988); and Joe Morehead, *Theory and Practice in Library Education: The Teaching-Learning Process* (Littleton, CO: Libraries Unlimited, 1980).

2. L. Houser and Alvin M. Schrader, *The Search for a Scientific Profession: Library Science Education in the U.S. and Canada* (Metuchen, NJ: Scarecrow Press, 1978).

3. Ups and downs of the transition are well-documented in Carl M. White, "Transition to University Standards," *A Historical Introduction to Library Education: Problems and Progress to 1951* (Metuchen, NJ: Scarecrow Press, 1976), pp. 224-268.

4. Elizabeth Futas, "The Practicum in Collection Development: A Debate," In *Recruiting, Educating, and Training Librarians for Collection Development*, Peggy Johnson and Sheila S. Intner, eds. (Westport, CT: Greenwood Press, 1994), pp. 145-156.

5. Ibid., p. 155.

6. The course is also open to doctoral students, many of whom are library directors, assistant directors, or department heads. Their greater knowledge and experience enable them to produce work that is often higher in quality and includes more detail than that of master's degree students, but it does not differ in kind.

7. Depending on the day of the week that a class is taught and a particular semester's holiday schedule, a four-credit course generally meets thirteen or fourteen times. Less often, it will meet for fifteen sessions, which is the maximum number possible.

8. See, for example, Richard Wood, "The Conspectus as a Collection Development Tool for College Libraries and Consortia," In *Acquisitions '90; Conference on Acquisitions, Budgets, and Collections; May 16 and 17, 1990, St. Louis, Missouri; Proceedings,* David C. Genaway, comp. And ed. (Canfield, OH: Genaway, 1990), pp. 413-434; or John H. Whaley, "Groping toward National Standards for Collection Evaluation," *Show-Me Libraries* 37 (March 1986): pp. 25-28.

APPENDIX A. Excerpts from the LIS 453 Syllabus, Fall 1999

INTRODUCTION

Much of what you learn in library school presumes the existence of collections of library materials. In this course, our attention is focused on the building, developing, and managing of collections. Naturally, collections don't grow in a vacuum. They are built by the acquisition and subsequent liquidation of materials. The holdings of any particular library are more-or-less dynamic: more, if it isn't part of the mission to preserve everything they acquire; less, if it is. Even archives grow and change, although they won't discard as much as some libraries do.

The processes of collection development and management include many facets and employ many skills. Most will sound familiar to students of management science:

- planning
- budgeting
- setting goals and objectives
- implementing plans
- evaluating results

In this class, each of these processes will be related to the collection. Planning will be done for future collections; goals and objectives will be set for them; budgeting and implementation will involve steps to reach the collection goals that have been set; evaluation of the job will end the cycle and cause it to begin again.

Each of you will choose a real library to use as a model for this course. Imagine yourself the newly hired collection development officer of your model library, responsible for building its collections. Your first task in this job is to develop a written collection development plan and go through the steps of implementing it. [If the library you choose already has a fully-developed policy statement <u>completed within the previous three years</u>, choose another library.] Assignments are designed to help you accomplish each phase of a complete collection development cycle. When you finish this class, you won't just have studied the process, you will have done it.

OBJECTIVES

When this course is completed, the student should be able to:

- determine the parameters of a library environment
- assess user needs for materials
- formulate collection goals and objectives
- evaluate existing collections
- allocate collection funds
- draw up a budget reflecting the desired allocations
- devise methods for selecting and deselecting materials
- write collection development and management policy documents.

ASSIGNMENTS

In this class, we assume you have just been hired by a library as their first collection development officer. Your first task is to create a collection development policy and procedure manual for the library. Select a real library to use as your model. If you wish to use a library that is too far away to visit in person, it is good, but you will need to know it well enough to describe it in detail without going there to make observations. If you currently are working in a library, you may use it, after asking permission from the director and your immediate supervisor (yes, both of them). If you are not working in a library at this time, choose a library that you can go to several times to gather information for the project (your local public library, your undergraduate college's library, Beatley Library, etc.). You must gather statistical data through observation or by extrapolating from publicly available reports, so a hypothetical institution will not do. And do not assume you should get the data by asking the librarians. You would not do that in the real world.

The term project is to create a fully-developed collecting manual for the library you have selected for your model. The manual is divided into sections that correspond to the assignments due at designated times during the semester. You will hand in each assignment twice: once on the due date given in the calendar, and, a second time as part of the final term project due on the penultimate day of class. When the assignment is handed in the first time, the instructor will review it and write critiques on the paper. Before it is handed in for the second and final time, you may revise it to address the instructor's criticisms. The term project will receive both a grade and a written evaluation.

All assignments are to be typed or word-processed, double-spaced, with wide margins (1 & 1/2" all around), following the instructions for theses of a standard style manual (e.g., the *University of Chicago Manual of Style*). Your assignments will be graded on their appearance, so be sure to format them as attractively and professionally as possible. Otherwise, you will lose points in the grade.

HAND IN ALL ASSIGNMENTS ON TIME. They are timed so you can complete the project by the end of the semester without killing yourself. If you are late, you will be penalized one grade (e.g., from A– to B+). Remember, the instructor needs time to review and evaluate everyone's documents, not just yours.

#1: IDENTIFY & DESCRIBE YOUR MODEL LIBRARY   DUE: 9/27/99
Choose your library. Begin with a formal identification of the library: its complete name, address, telephone number, email address, website URL, name of the director, and any other identifying data you believe is pertinent. Describe your library's mission, goals and objectives, its setting, physical plant, organization, staff, overall budget and other resources, and the people it serves. Describe the people who are being served in detail, naming the different types of users, the numbers in each group, and all other information you deem useful. If your library has published documents available, e.g., mission statements, floor plans, budgets, user analyses, etc., use them as source material. Do not hand in or reveal any confidential information.

#2: DESCRIBE THE LIBRARY'S PARENT BODY   DUE: 10/4/99
Prepare a complete description of your library's <u>parent body</u> (the college or university if it is an academic library; the company if it is a corporate library; the city or town if it is a public library, etc.). Give its mission, goals, and objectives (usually found in its charter, legislation, strategic plan, and other published reports), describe its setting, resources, organization, and all other details you deem pertinent. If you can obtain real documents that give this information, use them as source material for your report.

#3: SET COLLECTING GOALS AND OBJECTIVES   DUE: 10/18/99
Prepare a document giving the collection goals and objectives drawn up to serve the needs of your library for the forthcoming collecting cycle. They must be in harmony with the library's and the parent institution's mission, goals and objectives. Goals may be expressed in general terms (e.g., "increase mathematics literature"), but objectives must be written in <u>measurable</u> terms (e.g., increase mathematics literature by 10%), so that you can use them to evaluate your success or failure at the end of the collecting cycle.

#4: DESCRIBE CURRENT COLLECTION   DUE: 11/1/99
Prepare a profile of the existing collection. Identify each relevant division or department, each subject area, etc. Describe the number of titles and items in each category of material held, average age, condition, the balance among physical formats, between circulating and reference material, etc. If the collection is too large for you to examine each item, do a "quick and dirty" sampling, using the best method you can with the time and resources you have available.

#5: MEASURE COLLECTION QUALITY   DUE: 11/15/99
Prepare a written evaluation of the quality of the collection. You may compare titles held against a bibliography of recommended holdings, or against the catalog of a collection considered strong in the areas under consideration, or you may examine the use of materials compared to holdings in each area under consideration, or the rate at which user requests are filled, or a combination of these measures. Be sure to decide in advance what level of achievement will be considered "good" or "bad" and make your judgments explicit.

#6: PREPARE TO SELECT NEW MATERIALS   DUE: 11/22/99

Compile an annotated bibliography of the 10 best sources you will use or recommend to part-time selectors to select new materials for your collections. Do include important review journals, approval plans, gifts and exchanges, etc., and state how they will be used. Annotations should include the scope and coverage of the item, its frequency of issue, the number of expected reviews, and their particular value for the selector.

#7: ALLOCATE FUNDS   DUE: 11/29/99

Prepare a budget for purchases, giving the allocations you will allot for each category of material. It is useful to give a listing of the most recent allocations available (the current year's figures), the projected allocation ("next" year's figures), and the net change, arranged in three columns. It also is useful to see what percentage of the budget each allocation represents. Use sample budgets to help you format this assignment.

#8: GUIDE OTHER SELECTORS   DUE IN CLASS: 12/6/99

Write guidelines and policies for selection to be followed by part-time selectors under your management. [If you are the sole selector, prepare a written report describing the selection guidelines and policies you will follow, addressed to your director.] Include library policies on censorship and challenges to materials. Add a similar set of guidelines for removal of materials from the collections and decisions about replacement, remote storage, or disposal. [The guidelines should cover fundamental decisions, not mechanics, and should be intended for use by librarians, not support staff.]

#9: FINAL TERM PROJECT   DUE 12/13/99

Put your collection development policy and procedure manual together by combining the documents you have prepared for the ten assignments above, after revising them as you wish.

Add any material you believe is necessary to make the document easy to use on an ongoing basis, e.g., a procedure for reviewing and amending the policies/procedures, a table of contents, indexes or tabs, appendices, footnotes or endnotes (I have no preference–do whichever you like), and a bibliography of sources you used but did not cite anywhere in the body of the manual.

Remember, if you use the ideas you got from a source, you must footnote them wherever your paraphrases of their material appear or you are guilty of plagiarism. If you don't know what plagiarism is, consult the GSLIS Honor Code Policy statement, posted on the bulletin board outside the Dean's office (L-307).

Arrange the manual any way you wish, but assume it will become a permanent document for your library and will be used by staff, members of funding and governing bodies, patrons, etc.

GRADING

Final grades will be based on the term project (90%), and a combined grade (10%) for attendance, handing in assignments on time, and class participation.

Each assignment will receive a critique and a <u>provisional</u> grade. Students are expected to revise the documents to address the cricitisms and, thus, raise the final grades. The final term project will be evaluated according to the following schedule:

- completeness   20 points   (includes documentation, data, justifications, etc.)
- relevance   20 points   (appropriateness to the library, its users, etc.)
- ease of use   20 points   (can someone pick up your manual and use it?)
- format and style   20 points   (looks, readability, "professionalism")
- service potential   20 points   (will policies improve the collections?)

<u>Total points and letter grade equivalents</u>: 96-100 = A; 91-95 = A–; 86-90 = B+; 81-85 = B; 76-80 = B–; 71-75 = C+; 66-70 = C; 61-65 = D; 60 or below = F.

The professor will provide a written evaluation of the term project explaining where points were deducted and why.

Collection Development at SJU Libraries: Compromises, Missions, and Transitions

Lois Cherepon

Andrew Sankowski

SUMMARY. Collection development in academic libraries has become a difficult process in an era of technological change. Today's academic librarian must not only have subject expertise, but must also balance print and electronic collections, and have familiarity with budgeting skills such as a cost-benefit analysis. The creation and implementation of a Collection Development Policy Statement should be at the heart of all purchasing decisions. This statement should be a written policy, one which employs the ALA Guidelines of Collection Development and one that uses the university's and library's mission statements and strategic plan as its guiding force. The collection development policy needs to be revised in conjunction with the ever changing needs of the library's users and the growth of technology. This article will explore the creation and revision of the Collection Development Policy at St. John's University, New York. The focus is twofold: the need for a written Col-

Lois Cherepon is Associate Professor and Head of Reference Services, Loretto Memorial Library, St. John's University, 300 Howard Avenue, Staten Island, NY 10301 (E-mail: cherepol@stjohns.edu). Andrew Sankowski is Associate Professor and Head of Collection Development & Acquisitions Department, St. John's University Libraries, 8000 Utopia Parkway, Jamaica, NY 11439 (E-mail: sankowsa@stjohns.edu).

[Haworth co-indexing entry note]: "Collection Development at SJU Libraries: Compromises, Missions, and Transitions." Cherepon, Lois, and Andrew Sankowski. Co-published simultaneously in *The Acquisitions Librarian* (The Haworth Information Press, an imprint of The Haworth Press, Inc.) No. 30, 2003, pp. 63-75; and: *Collection Development Policies: New Directions for Changing Collections* (ed: Daniel C. Mack) The Haworth Information Press, an imprint of The Haworth Press, Inc., 2003, pp. 63-75. Single or multiple copies of this article are available for a fee from The Haworth Document Delivery Service [1-800-HAWORTH, 9:00 a.m. - 5:00 p.m. (EST). E-mail address: docdelivery@haworthpress.com].

http://www.haworthpress.com/store/product.asp?sku=J101
© 2003 by The Haworth Press, Inc. All rights reserved.
10.1300/J101v15n30_06

lection Development Policy Statement and the evolution of that statement at St. John's University. *[Article copies available for a fee from The
Haworth Document Delivery Service: 1-800-HAWORTH. E-mail address:
<docdelivery@haworthpress.com> Website: <http://www.HaworthPress.com> © 2003
by The Haworth Press, Inc. All rights reserved.]*

KEYWORDS. Collection development, academic libraries, transitions,
future of collection development, St. John's University

Collection development in the 21st century has become a balancing act
for academic librarians. Deciding what to purchase in electric format,
what to continue to purchase in print, and what to purchase in both formats becomes increasingly difficult during lean economic times and subsequent reductions in library budgets. The emphasis is decidedly toward,
whenever possible, making the migration to a virtual environment. However, this task becomes difficult when you factor into the formula the fact
that everything is not available in electronic format. Of those items that
are available electronically, sometimes the print versions are superior to
their electronic counterparts. And in other cases, the electronic version is
richer than the print version and may contain multi-media applications.
Print may be necessary due to usage, due to limitations of the hardware,
or due to the intricacies of the systems software at your institution. Furthermore, for many electronic databases, the emphasis is on current materials, rather than archival coverage. Electronic databases may discontinue
coverage of some of its contents, including coverage of articles from specific journals. How does the academic librarian accomplish the task at
hand, continue to develop a print collection, while simultaneously creating a virtual collection? The answer involves compromise, keeping current with both technology and resources, and creating or re-creating a
collection development policy statement that reflects both the library's
mission and the university's mission.

COMPROMISE

The fine art of compromise is a necessary component in today's collection development strategy. Most collections cannot be all inclusive in every subject area or every major offered by the university or college. How
will you choose to maintain the collections you currently own and what
percentage of the collection will you acquire electronically? In all areas,
from science to business to humanities, more and more resources are be-

coming available online, creating more choices and decisions in collection development. What is the university's policy towards the purchase of electronic resources? Will the university be able to support these electronic resources? Are other units of the university willing to concede that the library should not be expected to bear the brunt of the entire budget for these items? For example, would the school of business be willing to purchase a company and industry research product that costs over $20,000 per year? The costs of an online resource entail more than just the preliminary output of funding to purchase the item. The annual or renewal fees must be factored into the budget. Price increases are a given for many of these resources. Upgrading equipment, both computer hardware and peripherals such as printers, must also become part of the equation.

Collection development in today's academic library includes being able to analyze and support a budget as well as having the subject expertise to acquire the standard or basic materials for that field of study. Library liaisons should work with faculty to determine needs for their departments and discuss with them the possible purchase of materials in electronic formats. Collection development in today's academic library includes being able to acquire research materials, in addition the standard or basic materials for a specific area. Subject knowledge, computer savvy, and budgeting experience comprise the core skills of the 21st century collection development librarian. The term "compromise" is multi-faceted when referring to the complex world of collection development. The compromise is not just deciphering which collections will be developed and in what capacity, it is also a compromise of your time and energy. You need to devote as much time to the computer or technical aspects of the resources and to budget issues as you do to the subject material. Compromise becomes broad and all encompassing. The librarian compromises the time devoted to the process due to the many and varied demands he/she faces while evaluating and selecting materials. The University must compromise because they must select the avenue that their limited financial resources will allow them to follow. Finally, the library's collection can be compromised by the selection of one format over the other, electronic over print. This is especially true when, for the sake of a shrinking print budget, a title or series is cancelled and then replaced with an electronic product, which in some cases may not offer the same versatility or availability as the print version offered. This is the case when a CD-ROM product, which offers limited use unless it is networked, would only be available to a specified number of users, whereas the print counterpart, if multivolume, might be used by numerous users simultaneously.

THE LIBRARY/UNIVERSITY MISSION

How does the librarian know that the materials chosen and funds invested will further the mission of the library and the university? The answer to this question is both easy and difficult. You must know the mission of the institution and use that as your yardstick in making purchasing decisions. Your library should also have a strategic plan with specific objectives and goals outlined, as well as a library mission statement that reflects the university's mission, and use these tools as your primary guide. The absence of a library mission statement means the absence of a clear set of priorities. The library's mission statement will guide the creation and implementation of the collection development policy and assist the librarian in making difficult purchasing decisions. This is the relatively easy portion of the equation–a thorough knowledge of your mission. You also need to have a firm grasp of the objectives and goals of your library's strategic plan. The strategic plan, which by it's very nature will change more frequently than the mission statement, should play a key role in the development and maintenance of your collection policy. However, knowing and understanding the mission and strategic plan is not enough. You must also be able to interpret the mission statement and strategic plan in conjunction with the collection development policy, and apply your understanding and knowledge of these tools to the task at hand.

The librarian who is a multifaceted professional is able to weigh the consequences of purchasing something electronically while canceling the print version of that same resource. The difficulty of this task is evident. The selector must evaluate and purchase resources that fulfill the mission of the university and the library. The selector then needs to evaluate both the print and electronic versions of the resource. Based on usage and needs, they must determine which version should be chosen. If funds are available and usage warrants it, perhaps selecting both versions of the same resource is an option, as in the case of encyclopedias where a current print edition is needed for the reference collection but the university also wants to make it available online. In addition to deciding whether to select print or electronic (or both) versions, the selector must also determine whether or not the current technology will allow these materials to be stored, archived and accessed in the future. Many libraries that purchased materials on CD-ROM ten years ago can no longer use these materials due to changes in both hardware and software.

How do librarians keep track of all the new technological developments and products? In addition to the standard methods of keeping track of new developments, such as attending conferences and reading reviews, membership in a consortium can be an invaluable source of information and peer reviews. If the library is part of a consortium composed of several institutions, it can readily secure input and opinions concerning selection of electronic resources. The SJU Library, along with academic and public libraries from the area, is a member of the WALDO Consortium. WALDO's Database Committee is an extremely useful vehicle providing information and feedback in the collection development decision making process. Generally, the consortia is able to secure lower prices for subscriptions to databases.

HARD CHOICES–
IMPLEMENTING THE CDP IN AN ELECTRONIC WORLD

The task of implementing a collection development policy becomes an intricate and difficult one. The selector must be knowledgeable about the university and library's mission and strategic plan, must be able to evaluate resources based on changes in technology which have not yet occurred and stay abreast of the current trends, and finally must be able to implement all of these into a collection development policy. It is a daunting task which requires balancing several components simultaneously and implementing them while following something as complex as a collection development policy. More importantly, the selector must also determine if the investment in the resource warrants the expenditures of time and money. The ability to perform a cost-benefit analysis incorporating usage statistics analysis is, for all intents and purposes, a required skill among selectors if they hope to provide excellent resources for the collection within the framework of a shrinking budget and lightning speed technological changes. A cost-benefit analysis serves as a sound and objective basis for making tough financial decisions. Analyzing use statistics may not make collection development less difficult but it will provide the selector with rationale for choosing the resources and for recommending a particular format, print or online. Thus, the analysis of usage statistics provided by vendors of e-resources, including online databases, assists us in making informed decisions about retaining subscriptions to resources that are meeting the needs of our academic community. The usage reports allow the selectors to review many factors about subscription or product–frequency of use, time/date of usage, as well as how the product is being used (i.e., downloading or e-mailing information).

Other issues that need consideration when selecting a product include:

- Duplication of titles among different aggregator packages, which diminishes financial resources quickly
- Need to migrate from one electronic format to a new one (e.g., from CD-ROM version of a product and hardware needed to support that, to Web version of product)
- The possibility that some publishers are not willing to unbundle print from electronic subscriptions–and buying both can diminish financial resources more quickly
- "Outdated pricing models" that publishers currently offer–the scholarly community needs to push publishers in developing new models in providing access to e-resources (an interesting new development in the biomedical fields is the "Public Library of Science" movement to establish an online public library that would provide the full contents of published works in medicine and the life sciences in a freely accessible, fully searchable, interlinked form; http://www.publiclibraryofscience.org/plosFAQ.htm.
- The fact that there is an increasing number of free scholarly and/or statistical resources currently available through the U.S. Government, non-profit organizations, public companies, universities, and stock exchanges. One example is the Securities and Exchange Commission's Edgar Database. Economically challenged libraries may want to explore what is available free of charge before purchasing decisions are made for databases and other resources.

THE COLLECTION DEVELOPMENT POLICY STATEMENT

At St. John's University, the collection development policy is a written document, not an oral tradition. Some institutions still lack a written policy. In a 1993 survey of academic librarians conducted by Casserly and Hegg, it was found that 71.6% of respondents indicated that they have written policy statements. Richard Snow explains why some institutions continue to operate without a written policy. "One possible explanation for the absence of universal acceptance of the written policy, despite its near unanimous endorsement in librarianship's literature, is the lack of precise definition of what a written policy is as opposed to what it does. William A. Wortman illustrates this difficulty when he defines the written collection development policy as 'a crystallization of each library's understanding of how its collection can serve its mission.' He calls the policy a 'detailed profile of all the subjects in which the library will collect books, periodicals, and other materials or media' "(Snow, 191).

The collection development policy statement (CDPS) is defined as a statement which includes principal collection objectives of the library; it identifies purpose, direction, and philosophy; and is a pointer indicating which direction the collection is being developed. The purpose of the CDPS is to provide guidance for library faculty in selecting, weeding, and preserving materials, as well as other collection development and management activities, in order to ensure continuity and balance in collection growth. The advantages of a CDPS are that the statement helps all staff members focus on the library mission; it introduces the process conducive to gathering data and updating collection management strategies, and provides a sense of continuity. Without a CDPS in place, libraries would find it difficult to build consistently and exclusively on an oral tradition and a central rationale and plan would be missing. The Collection Development Policies Committee (CODES) of ALA's Reference and Adult Services Division cited to the importance of collection development policies in 1993, stating that collection development policy statements allow communication between the library and various constituencies throughout the university.

> Collection policy statements facilitate communication with several audiences. Primary users of the collections, including faculty, teachers, students, corporate staff, or members of the general community, constitute one essential audience . . . Library administrators, another critical audience, are concerned with the expenditure of acquisitions and 'information access' funds . . . Library consortia members . . . constitute another important audience. (RQ, 65)

At SJU the Collection Development Policy Committee prepared their document using the American Library Association's *Guide for Written Policy Statements* (1996) as their foundation document, with input from subject selectors and department heads. Each subject selector and department head was responsible for preparing a statement for his/her subject area(s). The policy for selection of both print and electronic resources was incorporated into the document. This document is continuously revised to reflect any changes in the library and the university curricula. According to Carol van Zijl, the Collection Development Policy Statement is "a document drawn up by a specific library to provide guidelines whereby the collection is developed and managed to meet the needs of that particular user group" (van Zijl, 100).

The components of the SJU Collection Development Policy Statement include: a description of the mission and organizational objectives; a description of the University community; identification of users served; the library's official stance on intellectual freedom, censorship, and copyright; a brief overview of the collection; the organization of collection management and development; budget structure and allocation policy; and cooperative collection development agreements. The policy for specific subjects includes: selection policy; types of material collected; languages collected; types of publications collected (e.g., monographs, microform, electronic); collection intensity levels; strengths and weaknesses of collections; and descriptions of depth and breadth of subject areas.

MIDDLE STATES AND REACCREDITATION

The most dramatic changes at St. John's University regarding collection development took place in 1994 during the library's self study in preparation for a Middle States Accreditation visit. During this time period, library administration appointed Middle States report subcommittees to explore various library issues, including curriculum, faculty development, cultural diversity in an interdependent world, and outcomes assessment. The impact of electronic formats was one area to be explored by the curriculum subcommittee. Through a survey, faculty and students evaluated and commented on library resources, including online and CD-ROM databases.

A major recommendation by the curriculum subcommittee was to "expand access to electronic information sources. This includes making the necessary technological enhancements and securing adequate budgetary support" (Middle States Report, 103). Additionally, the subcommittee reported that: "To insure that electronic access to information remains relevant to the teaching/learning process, a discussion of these resources needs to be a regular topic at collection management meetings" (Middle States Report, 99). Furthermore, "in order to move to the next level of delivering electronic information services, it is essential that the University install the infrastructure necessary to link the Libraries with other campus buildings and to provide the Libraries with access to the Internet" (p. 99). With this in mind, the library administration and faculty, in cooperation with Information Technology, worked on improving access to the Internet.

FACULTY INVOLVEMENT

An integral part of a CDPS is establishing and maintaining input from faculty regarding recommendations for new materials. Faculty are partners with the library in the collection development process. The liaison program enables librarians and faculty to exchange ideas in regard to curricula and needed materials for the library collection. Faculty need to be consulted and provided with information regarding the library collection and the selection process.

At SJU, there is an established library liaison program which promotes communication between library and teaching faculty. In 2000, the library administration appointed a Library Liaison Committee to re-evaluate and restructure the current library liaison activities. This committee, together with input from all library faculty, created a new list of liaison duties/responsibilities, a new set of guidelines, and a redesigned list of liaison assignments. Librarians were asked to serve as liaisons to various units, schools, and departments throughout the university. A major part of liaison responsibilities is to maintain an ongoing flow of communication with their assigned areas by making initial contact with the unit or department, offering to attend department meetings as a representative of the library, and providing information to faculty on new products and resources. A survey conducted at the University of Las Vegas Nevada indicates that faculty prefer the electronic mode of communicating with selectors. "When asked to share their thoughts on the best method for the library to let them know what was available in the library, most participants (in the survey) favored brief periodic electronic mail announcements" (Starkweather, 653).

Feedback about their liaison activities is shared with other library faculty and administrators via the library's listserv. The library's web site provides faculty with an additional means of participating in the selection of new acquisitions. Faculty have the opportunity to critique electronic resources and to make purchasing recommendations on the library's web page. The SJU library also has a trial databases page that is frequently updated. At library liaison meetings, this trial page is described and demonstrated for faculty. Input from faculty about selection of materials is vital. Felix T. Chu cites to the importance of "The Librarian-Faculty Relations in Collection Development," stating:

> It is assumed that librarians and faculty are in separate parts of the organization and neither has authority over the other. But for selected tasks such as collection development, the representatives

from the various units–librarians and faculty–must work together across hierarchical boundaries. Lacking appropriate authority, power emanates from influence based on specialized knowledge, trust, and other intangible factors. (Chu, 17)

Faculty suggestions for trial subscriptions are also taken under consideration.

DISTANCE EDUCATION

Distance learning programs offered at many colleges and universities throughout the country are major influences on the selection process for electronic resources. According to Richard J. Goodram and Don L. Bosseau, "there has been an accelerating development of distance education and distance learning programs. The 'virtual classroom' and the 'virtual campus' have been added to the 'virtual library' as models to support these programs . . . these programs both create and use Internet-based data resources" (Goodram, 155).

Students in distance education programs need to have access to as many resources as possible within a non-traditional setting. At institutions offering distance education programs, the number and the subject of program offered play a major role in purchasing decisions. Distance education students need to have full text access; examples of databases selected for a distance learning program may include EbscoHost, LEXIS/NEXIS Academic Universe, and Proquest Direct for journal articles and NetLibrary for books. If, however, the program is very specialized and only databases with citations and abstracts are available, these databases would need to be considered for purchase. Some examples of these specialized databases include: the MLA International Bibliography, Sociological Abstracts, and Criminal Justice Abstracts.

The SJU e-Reference service, "Ask a Librarian," adds another dimension of communication to distance learning. "Ask a Librarian," which became operational in March 2000, is open to SJU community members and to others outside of this community, and allows them to send questions, including reference and directional queries, to library faculty. Many of questions received through "Ask a Librarian" focus on the collection, both print and electronic. Through these various endeavors, the Library is moving toward a virtual environment and enhancing the growth of the distance learning program on campus.

CONCLUSION

To summarize, the SJU Libraries have moved from a largely print environment to a virtual environment. The addition of electronic resources to the range of materials available for purchase has made the job of selectors more complex. To facilitate effective collection development of both print and electronic resources, the library has followed the mission statement of the University and has prepared a written policy statement. The catalyst for change was the 1994 Self-Study report, prepared for our Middle States visit, by library faculty and administrators. Since the preparation of this document, the library and university have developed a library site and have implemented electronic database remote access, distance education programs, and expanded e-reference. Undoubtedly, more technological breakthroughs will be part of our future; with collection guidelines in place, we will be prepared to face them.

At St. John's University, both print resources and electronic resources are purchased. There is, however, a growing demand for more resources supporting the virtual classroom. We established a written CDPS, rooted by our library and university mission statements and our strategic plan, which undergoes revisions as needed. The library has incorporated new means of gathering acquisitions suggestions from faculty and other users through the Trial Database web page and the newly established e-reference service. We have also focused on improving communication with teaching faculty via a re-designed liaison program. As we have weathered transitions from a mostly print collection to a combined print and e-based collection, we have tried to maintain our sense of mission throughout the many financial and format compromises.

The challenge for the future is to continue to develop our library's collections in a world where technology is becoming simultaneously commonplace and complex. We will continue to develop new methods of incorporating into our selection process input from our faculty and other users. Edward Shreeves identifies the increased emphasis on user input stating that " . . . the function of selection will likely pass more and more into the hands of the users, who will exploit the tools provided by libraries and others to identify and retrieve material through the network. Collection development administrators will likely become managers of electronic rights, ensuring that the avenues are open for the users of his or her institution to get to the information they need" (Shreeves, 386). We will also continue to explore shared access to library collections via consortia efforts and other collaborations. Along with the transitions and compromises, we need to revise our mission as our needs change while using that mission as an anchor for our decision making. New levels of shared collection development ventures need to be explored if we hope to expand our collection in an era of tight budgets and swiftly changing technology.

BIBLIOGRAPHY

American Library Association. *Guide for Written Collection Policy Statements.* 2nd ed. Chicago, Ill.: American Library Association, 1996.

Balas, Janet I. "Developing Library Collections for a Wired World." *Computers in Libraries* 20 (June 2000): 61-3.

Chu, Felix T. "Librarian-Faculty Relations in Collection Development." *Journal of Academic Librarianship* 23 (January 1997): 15-20.

Davis, Trisha L. "The Evolution of Selection Activities for Electronic Resources." *Library Trends* 45 (Winter 1997): 391-403.

Foster, Janet. "Collection Development, from Text to Technology." *Computers in Libraries* 20 (June 2000): 34-9.

Goodram, Richard J. and Don L. Bosseau et al. "Cooperation or Competition: An Entrepreneurial Question?" *Journal of Academic Librarianship* 24 (March 1998): p.155.

Holleman, Curt. "Electronic Resources: Are Basic Criteria for the Selection of Materials Changing?" *Library Trends* 48 (Spring 2000): 694-710.

Intner, Sheila S. "The Ostrich Syndrome: Why Written Collection Development Policies are Important." *Technicalities* 16 (July/August 1996): 1+.

Johnson, Margaret Ann. "Collection Policies for Electronic Resources." *Technicalities* 18 (June 1998): p. 10-2.

LaGuardia, Cheryl and Stella Bentley. "Electronic Databases: Will Old Collection Development Policies Still Work?" *Online* (July 1992): 60+.

Metz, Paul. "Principles of Selection for Electronic Resources." *Library Trends* 48 (Spring 2000): 711-28.

Miller, Ruth H. "Electronic Resources and Academic Libraries, 1980-2000: A Historical Perspective." *Library Trends* 48 (Spring 2000): 645-70.

"The Relevance of Collection Development Policies: Definition, Necessity, and Applications." *RQ* 33 (Fall 1993): 65-74.

Shreeves, Edward. "The Acquisitions Culture Wars. (electronic and printed library resources)." *Library Trends* 48 (Spring 2000): 877-90.

Shreeves, Edward. "Is there a future for cooperative collection development in the digital age? (Resource Sharing in a Changing Environment)." *Library Trends* 45 (Winter 1997): 373-90.

Snow, Richard. "Wasted Words: The Written Collection Development Policy and the Academic Library." *Journal of Academic Librarianship* 22 (May 1996): 191-94.

St. John's University Library. *Self-Study Report.* Jamaica, N.Y.: St. John's University Library, 1994.

Starkweather, Wendy M. and Camille Clark Wallin. "Faculty Response to Library Technology: Insights on Attitudes." *Library Trends* 47 (Spring 1999): p. 640-68.

Strauch, Katina. "Don't Get Mired in It: Make Some Bricks." *Journal of Academic Librarianship* 18 (March 1992): p. 12.

Strong, Rob. "A Collection Development Policy Incorporating Electronic Formats." *Journal of Interlibrary Loan, Document Delivery & Information Supply* 9 (1999): p. 53-64.

Svenningsen, Karen and Lois H. Cherepon. "Revisiting Library Mission Statements in the Era of Technology." *Collection Building* 17 (1998): 16-9.

Terry, Ana Arias. "How Today's Technology Affects Libraries' Collection Choices." *Computers in Libraries* 20 (June 2000): 51-5.

Thornton, Glenda A. "Impact of Electronic Resources on Collection Development, the Roles of Librarians, and Library Consortia." *Library Trends* 48 (Spring 2000): 842-56.

Van Zijl, Carol. "The Why, What, and How of Collection Development Policies." *South African Journal of Library and Information Science.* 66 (September 1998): 99+.

Williams, James F. II. "Rationing Resources in a Reconceptualized Environment." *Journal of Academic Librarianship* 18 (March 1992): p. 15-16.

Collection Management Statements on the World Wide Web

Joseph Straw

SUMMARY. This article surveyed the web pages of 124 libraries that are members of the Association of Research Libraries (ARL). The survey was looking to find collection policies or statements that might be available from the web pages of ARL libraries. The examination was hoping to find different examples of collection management statements that would range from the very detailed to nothing at all. It's hoped that the information gathered in this article will show the extent that major research institutions communicate collection management information using the electronic medium. *[Article copies available for a fee from The Haworth Document Delivery Service: 1-800-HAWORTH. E-mail address: <docdelivery@haworthpress.com> Website: <http://www.HaworthPress.com> © 2003 by The Haworth Press, Inc. All rights reserved.]*

KEYWORDS. Collection management statements, academic libraries, World Wide Web, public information, Internet

INTRODUCTION

Collection management is one of the most basic and important functions in the library. The collection management policy is vitally impor-

---

Joseph Straw is Associate Professor of Library Administration, University of Illinois at Urbana-Champaign (E-mail: jstraw@uiuc.edu).

[Haworth co-indexing entry note]: "Collection Management Statements on the World Wide Web." Straw, Joseph. Co-published simultaneously in *The Acquisitions Librarian* (The Haworth Information Press, an imprint of The Haworth Press, Inc.) No. 30, 2003, pp. 77-86; and: *Collection Development Policies: New Directions for Changing Collections* (ed: Daniel C. Mack) The Haworth Information Press, an imprint of The Haworth Press, Inc., 2003, pp. 77-86. Single or multiple copies of this article are available for a fee from The Haworth Document Delivery Service [1-800-HAWORTH, 9:00 a.m. - 5:00 p.m. (EST). E-mail address: docdelivery@haworthpress.com].

http://www.haworthpress.com/store/product.asp?sku=J101
© 2003 by The Haworth Press, Inc. All rights reserved.
10.1300/J101v15n30_07

tant in guiding the library in their efforts to select and acquire material. In the past, as well as today, written collection management statements have often been suggested as a way for libraries to rationally plan the direction of their collection building. With the advent of the Internet, opportunities for libraries to disseminate collection policy information are almost unlimited. Despite the possibilities, the extent in which libraries use the Internet to communicate their overall collection policies is still not widely known. This article will examine the web pages of the Association of Research Libraries (ARL) members to see the extent to which premier research institutions provide collection policy information through the vehicle of the Internet. It's hoped that the information gathered in this article will show the extent that written collection policies have migrated to the Internet, and provide a sense of the kinds of collection information that's available to the public electronically.

REVIEW OF THE LITERATURE

The literature in collection management strongly endorses the idea of thoughtful collection policies. Many writers have insisted on the need for formal written documents that frame the objectives, budgeting, and workload of building a library collection. The American Library Association insists that written policies can be a "necessary tool" that: "defines the scope of existing collections and maps the future development of collections."[1] Mary J. Bostic describes the written policy as a way for libraries to consider the "the long- and short-term needs of the community it serves."[2] In recommending the RLG conspectus in developing policy statements, Dora Biblarz contends that taking a detailed approach will help to identify the "hills and valleys" of a given library collection.[3] Marion Buzzard advises that the realities of budgets and space in libraries dictates the need for a written policy so the library can be properly placed as institutions compete for scarce resources.[4] Perhaps one of the strongest justifications comes from Anthony Ferguson when he writes that written policies "force the selector to thoroughly think through the issues and put down on paper what purpose will bind their decisions."[5]

While many people in the literature have sung the praises of written collection policies, others have pointed out that in actual practice many libraries have failed to commit policies to paper. A 1977 study of 70 ARL libraries found that only 30 (29%) had developed written statements.[6] Bonita Bryant in surveying medium sized academic libraries found that 25 percent had no written policy and another 42 percent had incomplete or only draft documents.[7] In 1988 a self selected survey of 193 small to medium sized libraries found that 58 percent had some kind of written policy and these varied from detailed documents to one-page mission statements.[8] Another 1988 examination of five research libraries in Alabama, found that only one had a written collection policy while the others cited lack of money, time, and manpower as reasons for not developing a policy.[9] Whether justifying the need for a written policy or pointing out the large number of libraries that have no policy, the literature has not explored the impact of new Internet technologies on the articulation of collection development policy.

ASSOCIATION OF RESEARCH LIBRARIES (ARL)

A logical starting place to look at collection policies would be the member institutions of the Association of Research Libraries. ARL is a non-profit organization of the top libraries in North America that has advocated for research institutions in the areas of access, scholarship, and information policy. The current ARL membership is made up of 124 institutions of different types. Academic and university libraries make up the bulk of the association with 114 members with national libraries the second largest group with four. Public libraries are represented by three members and a research institute, consortium, and a state library each have one member. Membership in ARL is strongly based on the size and depth of collections. The main criteria for membership consists of the number of volumes held, number of volumes added, periodical or serial subscriptions, overall library budget, and numbers of professional staff. ARL libraries have very broad interdisciplinary collections consisting of different materials in a wide variety of formats and languages. Whether taken individually or as a whole, the collections that make up the ARL membership are some of the finest in the world.[10]

LOOKING AT ARL WEB PAGES

This study examines the web pages of ARL member libraries to identify available collection policy information. This examination is hoping to identify:

- A collections or acquisitions website
- A comprehensive collection policy statement that may follow the ALA Guidelines for Written Collection policy or some other conspectus approach.

- A non-comprehensive collection statement that outlines the collection and points out strengths but does not give a detailed profile of all collection areas.
- A stand alone mission statement that appears without a comprehensive or non-comprehensive collection statement.
- Institutions that have no collection information at all.

The mission and policy statements gathered will be the ones that focus on the collection as a whole and will exclude ones that describe the holdings of library units or subject collections.

LIMITATIONS OF THIS EXAMINATION

Only ARL members will be examined, so the great majority of academic and public libraries will not be included. Since this examination is only looking at overall collection policies, unit or subject collections falling outside of a library wide policy will also be excluded. The focus on Internet collection materials will not allow for comparison with internal written documents that may or may not exist at ARL libraries. Given these limitations, any general statement about the way ARL or library institutions in general think about collection development will clearly be limited.

RESULTS OF THIS EXAMINATION–
COLLECTIONS OR ACQUISITIONS PAGES

The collections or acquisitions page can serve as a gateway for a library that may wish to mount collection management information on a web page. These pages can provide clear links to collection management documents and provide contact information to individuals who have responsibility for the collection. Of the 124 ARL web sites that were examined, 88 had links to a collections or acquisitions site representing 71% of the total. These 88 sites varied greatly in quality and content. Of these 88 sites, 64 (73%) had links or access to some kind of collection development information. This could be anything from a detailed comprehensive policy to a stand alone mission statement. A group of 24 libraries (27%) had a collections or acquisitions page but contained no collection management information. These 24 sites contained very minimal information mostly consisting of very brief facts about the collection or simply departmental location or contact information.

COMPREHENSIVE COLLECTION POLICY STATEMENTS

The comprehensive written collection policy represents the most detailed and analytical way that a library can describe its collection building efforts. Of the 124 library pages examined, 37 have access to comprehensive collection policy statements representing 30% of the ARL total. In their collection policy web pages, all of these 37 institutions use some variation of a conspectus approach to collection evaluation and description. A conspectus approach looks at the extent and depth of library collections in a very systematic fashion. Collection development statements using a conspectus model have been used to create the paper versions of comprehensive policies for many years. The American Library Association in talking about written statements defines the conspectus as:

> A comprehensive survey: a tabulation of particulars representing a general view of them. The term used here means an overview or summary of collection strengths and collecting intensities, arranged by subject, classification scheme, or a combination of either, and containing standardized codes for collection or collecting levels and languages of materials collected. Such a conspectus is a synopsis of a library's collection or of a consortium's or network's coordinated collection development overview or policy.[11]

Guides established by the Research Libraries Group (RLG) and Pacific Northwest Conspectus Database (PNW) are used, with considerable local variation, by most of the 37 libraries with detailed collection policies on the web. The ARL libraries that have chosen to display comprehensive online collection statements are using techniques that have been used to make the same documents in paper.

A very important central feature of the conspectus driven model are the statements of collecting levels. All of the 37 libraries with detailed statements online have such a breakdown. These statements consist of a subject analysis, often by classification, of established strengths, formats, languages, and collecting intensities. The collecting intensities are often labeled into basic categories as defined by the RLG conspectus as:

1. Out of Scope–the library collects nothing on a topic.
2. Minimal Level–the library collects little beyond very basic works.
3. Basic Level–the library collects enough to outline the parameters of a topic but little else.

4. Instructional Level–the library collects enough material on a topic to treat it in some detail but falls short of providing collections that can support detailed research.
5. Research Level–the library provides material to provide detailed and systematic treatment of a topic.
6. Comprehensive Level–all items of recorded knowledge are collected for a defined topic or area.[12]

Many of the ARL libraries spell out these categories and often provide sub-categories that further describe their local collections. Numbering systems and icons are also used to describe and illuminate these basic categories.

The conspectus approach is often recommended as an ideal for writing a collection development policy. In talking about academic libraries, Marion Buzzard praises such an approach when she says:

> Libraries with written policy statements which are both comprehensive and detailed will find that many benefits accrue immediately. The librarian selectors emerge from the experience with a much better understanding of the nature of the academic programs, and of the materials they should be acquiring, and this information can be communicated to the faculty and the users. The existence of specific guidelines makes it easier to justify the acquisition or exclusion of certain types of materials and establish equity among a variety of disciplines and programs. A written policy greatly facilitates the training of new selectors and eases the period of transition. It is also a useful element in evaluating the strengths and weaknesses of existing collections.[13]

This examination would seem to suggest that many libraries are falling short in using the Internet to meet the lofty ideals of having a detailed policy. Many earlier studies have pointed out the reluctance of many libraries to commit detailed policies to paper. The fact that only 37 or 30% of 124 ARL libraries have detailed policies displayed electronically, would seem to suggest that like print a majority of libraries have not committed comprehensive statements to their web pages.

NON-COMPREHENSIVE COLLECTION STATEMENTS

The non-comprehensive collection policy statement is a more concise way for a library to describe the extent of its collections. Of the 124 libraries examined, 25 (21%) have a non-comprehensive statement on their web pages. Often called a narrative statement, these policies sketch out the parameters of a library collection but do not provide a detailed profile of collecting areas. In many cases, they can point out strengths and provide a sense of the subjects or clienteles served by the library.

The non-comprehensive or narrative statement can be formal or informal and can include a wide variety of information. In writing formal statements, it is recommended that they include a mission statement that outlines the purpose of the collection in the broadest sense. It is also suggested that the scope of coverage be defined which would identify the types of materials that are included or excluded. Subject strengths are also important to define, with some statement of the department or individual that's ultimately responsible for the collection.[14]

The 25 ARL libraries with non-comprehensive statements online, tend to be less formal with considerable differences in quality and content. They closely follow existing print documents (with many being PDF files of current written statements) and are strongly geared to local conditions and circumstances. A few even use a combination of conspectus outlines in their narrative statements to profile collection strengths or limited special collections of defined local importance.

STAND ALONE MISSION STATEMENTS

A stand alone mission statement can define a library's collection focus in a very general sense. All of the ARL libraries with comprehensive and non-comprehensive policies have some kind of statement of mission or purpose. A group of eight (7%) of the 124 libraries examined only had a mission statement on the web. These statements appear without any comprehensive, non-comprehensive, or any other collection information. All of these mission statements are local creations that give the most limited introduction possible to the library collection. Clearly this is an approach of a minority of libraries, and most libraries that have put collection information on their web pages have chosen to include a comprehensive or narrative statement as part of the total package.

NO COLLECTION STATEMENTS

A very large group of 54 ARL libraries (44%) have not put any collection statements on their web pages. It has been suggested that earlier studies have pointed out the large number of libraries that have not put collection development policies in writing. Some of the reasons that have been put forth are lack of resources, time, funding, and staffing. Clearly, many of these same factors are at work in libraries that have chosen not to put collection information on their web pages.

Priorities defined by the electronic medium must also be suggested as possible reasons for libraries failing to have collection development information on the web. Library web pages are a very dynamic way for users to access library resources. Online catalogs, article databases, electronic texts, and access to the open Internet are all possible from the 124 examined web pages. All of these sites are organized as information gateways that have an emphasis on connecting users to information they may need at a particular time. This information gathering or reference purpose is clearly the priority in the design and look of these ARL web sites. Even libraries that have detailed collection information, often have it buried deep within their sites and sometimes considerable efforts have to be made to call up the information. Why does a library collect in a certain way? Why are certain materials favored over others? These and other esoteric questions are clearly secondary in deciding what is mounted on library web pages.

The unique features of many ARL libraries may explain why collection policy information is absent from web pages. ARL libraries have some of the largest collections in the world containing millions of items in dozens of formats and languages. The parameters of some of these collections have been painstakingly established over decades and in some cases centuries. The task of surveying and analyzing such complex collections may be beyond the descriptive powers of existing collection management tools. In such cases, it's not surprising that libraries may not extend collection management information to their web pages.

Many ARL libraries also have many collections that are separated from main and central library locations. Organization by subject libraries is a common pattern across many ARL libraries. Many of these subject libraries have strong traditions of local autonomy in management and collection building. This autonomy is often reflected in collection policies that are different than those of the library as a whole. For some of the larger ARL libraries, dozens of collection management policies are often carried out without any central direction. In such places, it would not be surprising to find that an overall collection statement would not be found on their web pages.

CONCLUSION

Collection management statements have clearly been impacted by the advent of the Internet. This examination of ARL web pages has shown that many libraries have chosen to make available collection development information through the vehicle of the Internet. The choice to put out such information is by no means universal or uniform. Of the web sites that were looked at, 57% had some type of collection management statement that ranged from a thoughtful detailed policy to a single sentence mission statement. This left a large number of libraries with no collection information that could be found on their web pages. This result is similar to what earlier studies have found looking at traditional written policies. The libraries that have mounted either comprehensive policies or non-comprehensive statements have closely followed the forms that have been used to make existing written documents (in many cases the web versions were just scanned or PDF versions of print statements). Clearly the use of the Internet to communicate collection management information is in its infancy, and much still needs to be expanded and refined. The opportunities created by Internet technology have the potential to allow libraries to disseminate information about their collections to much wider audiences, and create the chance for real collaboration with users in developing refined collections that everyone can use.

REFERENCES AND NOTES

1. American Library Association. *Guide for Collection Policy Statements*. (Chicago: American Library Association, 1989), pp. 2.

2. Bostic, Mary J., "A Written Collection Policy: To Have and Have Not," *Collection Management* 10 No.3/4 (1988): 89-103.

3. Biblarz, Dora, "The Conspectus as Blueprint for Creating Collection Development Policy Statements," in *Collection Assessment* edited by Richard Wood and Katrina Strauch, (New York: The Haworth Press, Inc., 1992), pp.169-176.

4. Buzzard, Marion, "Writing a Collection Development Policy for an Academic Library," *Collection Management* 2 No. 4 (1978): 317-328.

5. Ferguson, Anthony W., "Interesting Problems Encountered On My Way To Writing an Electronic Information Collection Development Statement," *Against the Grain* 7 (April, 1995): 16-19, 90.

6. Association of Research Libraries. Office of Management Studies, *SPEC Kit 38: Collection Development Policies* (Washington, D.C.: Association of Research Libraries, Nov. 1977), pp. 1.

7. Bryant, Bonita, "Collection Development Policies in Medium-Sized Academic Libraries," *Collection Building* 2 (1980-1981): 6-26.

8. Theresa Taborsky and Patricia Lenkowski, *Collection Development Policies for College Libraries: Clip Note # 11* (Chicago: American Library Association, 1989), pp.1-2.

9. Linda McNair Cohen, "Collection Development in Alabama's Academic Libraries," *Collection Management* 10 no.3/4 (1988): 43-53.

10. Association of Research Libraries, *ARL Member Libraries.* ARL website <http://www.arl.org/members.html> Accessed: 10-21-02.

11. American Library Association, Guide, pp. 22.

12. Research Libraries Group, Inc. *RLG Collection Development Manual* (Stanford California: RLG, 1981), pp. 2.

13. Buzzard, "Writing a Collection Development Policy for an Academic Library," 325-326.

14. American Library Association, Guide, pp. 11.

Acquisitions Policy for Contemporary Topics in an Academic Library: Managing the Ephemeral

Ashley Robinson

SUMMARY. Acquisition of materials about contemporary topics is a matter of course for selectors in academic settings, yet written policy in that realm is difficult to locate. Considerations important to the selection process are discussed and a suggested policy statement is included. *[Article copies available for a fee from The Haworth Document Delivery Service: 1-800-HAWORTH. E-mail address: <docdelivery@haworthpress.com> Website: <http://www.Haworth Press.com> © 2003 by The Haworth Press, Inc. All rights reserved.]*

KEYWORDS. Contemporary topics, acquisitions

INTRODUCTION AND BACKGROUND

Penn State's University Libraries have long had a strong collection development framework that provides a wide range of documents in support of materials selectors. These include guidelines and policy statements as well as materials relating to management, the entire ac-

Ashley Robinson is Gateway Librarian, The Pennsylvania State University Libraries, 102 Paterno Library, University Park, PA (E-mail: axr23@psulias.psu.edu).

[Haworth co-indexing entry note]: "Acquisitions Policy for Contemporary Topics in an Academic Library: Managing the Ephemeral." Robinson, Ashley. Co-published simultaneously in *The Acquisitions Librarian* (The Haworth Information Press, an imprint of The Haworth Press, Inc.) No. 30, 2003, pp. 87-100; and: *Collection Development Policies: New Directions for Changing Collections* (ed: Daniel C. Mack) The Haworth Information Press, an imprint of The Haworth Press, Inc., 2003, pp. 87-100. Single or multiple copies of this article are available for a fee from The Haworth Document Delivery Service [1-800-HAWORTH, 9:00 a.m. - 5:00 p.m. (EST). E-mail address: docdelivery@haworthpress.com].

http://www.haworthpress.com/store/product.asp?sku=J101
© 2003 by The Haworth Press, Inc. All rights reserved.
10.1300/J101v15n30_08

quisitions and technical services process, and standards for individual units within the Libraries that wish to create their own policy statements and web-based information pages. Few individual units have posted their own acquisitions policies as the umbrella statement is intelligent, strong, and flexible, so there may be no perceived compelling reason or requirement for subject groups to do so. Nevertheless, some units have developed policies that further define and specify the scope and mission of the collection in those areas beyond more general statements. These subject-specific policies are intended to inform any reader and contribute to the development goals of the Libraries. They also succeed in laying out the intellectual considerations and processes that drive collection development in those focused areas, and they discuss selection sources, materials, and procedures. They are therefore valuable on several levels. This article examines the process of identifying and selecting materials dealing with contemporary topics, looks at criteria for writing a collection development statement, and suggests a formal collection development policy statement for this part of the collection.

WHY "CONTEMPORARY TOPICS" AND WHY BOTHER WITH A WRITTEN POLICY?

The Gateway Library is a rather odd duck within the Libraries as it is not a subject library and does not have its own collection. It is an all-electronic facility featuring twenty-four library computers, an instructional lab, and a continuously staffed service desk–an outgrowth of the old reference desk. The Gateway's primary responsibilities are instruction, outreach, reference, and information packaging. It is often the first stop for people new to the Libraries and offers a friendly, relaxed introduction to the mysteries and magic of the university library. One-on-one instruction is available, and many patrons take advantage of this as it provides the opportunity for non-threatening face-to-face personal tutoring, a human connection to millions of cataloged materials and vast amounts of other information that can easily overwhelm those new to the system. The adjacent Gateway lab of sixteen computers, teaching station, and data projector is in constant demand as a venue for small class instruction, including classes that introduce library resources to anyone in the entire community who shows up.

Students in introductory courses in rhetoric and composition and in speech communications typically seek just-in-time information and instruction in the Gateway as they attack those freshman writing assignments, which usually center around topics of interest to beginning students. Because we serve so many incoming first-year students, the Gateway staff librarians are selectors for library materials dealing with contemporary topics, typically the subject matter for first-year papers and projects as well as leisure reading. Even though we have no print collection within our unit, our exposure to student assignments positions us to be selectors of contemporary materials in support of the curriculum. Setting down a selection policy for Contemporary Topics has been a useful exercise in clarifying this charge and in defining potential acquisitions.

Actually developing an acquisitions policy for Contemporary Topics is like attempting to herd snakes: few traditional conditions or guidelines apply, and getting a grip on a sensible development policy is a slippery venture. It is not a development area mentioned in most academic library policy statements. For those whose collection development responsibilities include this area, having a stated policy could provide a framework for acquisitions as well as continued conversations about the scope and focus of this part of the collection, so it is a job worth doing.

CONTEMPORARY TOPICS
AS A FOCUS FOR DEVELOPMENT

Part of the problem involved in managing a contemporary topics collection lies in defining the term. Considering various topics that are current or modern can involve those that may also be referred to as Contemporary Issues, Current Events, News, Pop Culture, Popular Fiction or others. These titles frequently also link to other university courses offered, and that can present a set of ready-made connections to materials in support of curricula. However, the larger inclusive term covers topics that, while certainly contemporary, appeal to younger students by relating more closely to their lives than to the larger world. These students may be aware of what's going on out there, but that awareness has been filtered by media tilted toward adolescents. They are also brand-new to university life and are irresistibly drawn to wanting to write about fraternities, alcohol use on campus, and local crime statistics–topics that would never have occurred to them a few months earlier. They are frequently interested in persons and events (rappers, heavy-metal concerts) that many reference and acquisitions librarians know little or nothing about and about whom/which little lucid written material exists. Beginning students frequently know little about anything outside the current timeframe. Still, these students and their research assignments drive acquisitions in support of their research, which, in its way, is just as valuable as upper level academic research. Upper level academic researchers have to start somewhere, so we need to provide the best we can for emerging researchers in order to launch them successfully. At the same time, they provide the opportunity for us librarians to expand and to try to raise the level of this research through the judicious choice of support materials.

LITERATURE REVIEW

Penn State's Libraries Selectors Manual includes a number of collection development policy statements from other institutions as well as those few written by subject area specialists at our university, a good place to start this process through review of wheels already invented. A review of the literature posted in house and beyond indicates that Contemporary Topics is not an area usually identified for development in policy and acquisitions statements or writings related to them. A search of the *OCLC FirstSearch Library Lit* database returns three titles, none of which relates to contemporary topics as defined and all published prior to 1989. Changing keywords to "issues" and "contemporary" yields more results (28) but no more relevancy. Bibliographic instruction in Russia in 1992, contemporary issues in collection development in Nigeria in 1995, and Contemporary Australian issues are not useful in this context. Similar keyword combinations yielded no pertinent results. Searches in *ProQuest* and *Science Direct* were no more productive in this direction, but several articles appeared dealing with electronic sources of current information that could directly support research. During the past five years, *The Acquisitions Librarian* published no articles on or related to selection of Contemporary Topics materials. Examination of the acquisitions policy statements of the Big Ten schools' libraries available yielded no mention of Contemporary Topics or of any of its subsets, nor did those of several other selected libraries. It does not appear in lists of subject specialists or liaisons. The Michigan State Library Special Collections Division does include popular culture, radical and minority history, and comic books and strips, all of which could be considered contemporary topics but which are far more limited in scope. Many schools, including the University of North Carolina and Notre Dame, list courses such as physical education and anthropology that look at cultural studies, global issues, and Afro American contemporary issues, which indicates that the need for suitable materials exists but is not stated as such. Approval plans do not provide materials specifically to be examined under that or similar headings because of the difficulty in setting inclusive subject headings and ranges. Apparently, those dealing with this part of their collections are on their own, and this is another reason to craft an acquisitions policy statement and to make it available to others who might be wrestling with similar issues, especially if a requirement to do so exists. There's certainly no glamour in reinventing this particular wheel.

COLLABORATION

Collaboration with other librarians is also essential within the institution. "Role of the Selector" guidelines mention cooperative collection development possibilities in working with faculty and developing appropriate research collections at various campuses and among consortia members. This is an especially relevant consideration for Gateway's selectors as materials selected under Contemporary Topics find their homes all over the library system because they are not subject specific. As the Gateway Library does not have its own collection, everything it selects is actually housed in other subject areas. Checking for possible duplication of orders is therefore especially valuable. It is also useful to communicate to subject library librarians the research interests of beginning students, both to alert them to possible interactions with these students and to engage their help in identifying titles to acquire. In our case, as our Libraries serve one university geographically dispersed over twenty-four campuses, it is also wise to communicate regularly with librarians at other campus locations, many of whom share in the development of teaching materials, tutorials for databases, and similar ventures. Collection maintenance post-acquisition is normally part of a selector's responsibility, but this task transfers to the subject librarians in the parts of the libraries which actually house materials selected, so it is smart to have buy-in from those people, especially for items that might be viewed as lighter-weight than those normally chosen for research libraries. Decisions regarding retention or possible annexing are usually made by the subject librarians. These decisions might depend upon the condition of materials as time passes, another factor that could influence selection.

IDENTIFYING TOPICS AND TITLES

Several conditions apply to identifying titles for acquisition. First, topics about which information is needed must be identified. Then, materials answering students' needs must be located and decisions made regarding the suitability of the materials before they are acquired. Because these materials may be produced just-in-time to meet a market demand before the public moves on to the next thing, care must be taken to evaluate items for suitability for an academic library, both in content and in presentation.

Identifying current topics is an ongoing process. Keeping the usual file of announcements of forthcoming materials identifies new resources or new formats for old favorites, such as on-line versions of traditionally print materials. Gateway may in some cases contribute acquisitions funds to those of others to enable database purchase. Course packets and syllabi provide specific assignments in rhetoric and composition and speech communications: exploring issues, definition, argument, evaluation, and the like. This information often suggests research topics to students which they frequently accept rather than coming up with their own. It can be useful for selectors to acquire and be familiar with as many course packets for these classes as possible as each instructor presents the course as s/he individually structures it. Librarians also learn about students' interests during instruction sessions, either through discussion or through working with students during hands on portions of lessons. Campus events and local interest are the subjects of some writing assignments and may suggest purchase of materials by local writers and publishers. *Time* magazine, *U.S. News and World Report*, *Newsweek*, and even *People* can suggest world, national, and sometimes local events that are newsworthy or are milestones of some kind. Popular media, including television and movies, can send selectors searching for materials about Frida Kahlo, Area 51, or anything else popular for the moment.

Since students go to the Internet first, as a matter of course, it is useful to check frequently the topics most popular at the time. Google, probably the most popular searching tool, keeps lists of the keywords most frequently searched and returns nearly three mission hits in a search for "hot topics." Jeeves I.Q. presents the top searches conducted on Ask Jeeves, which means millions of searches conducted each day. CyberAtlas' site contains an amazing array of statistics and other easily accessed information about Internet searching and searchers that includes a myriad of other sources as well. Alexa.com, now associated with Amazon, adds to the staggering array, and frequently has analyses of happenings in the world of information. Top sites are ranked and numbers of hits noted by AJR Newslink. Searchengine Watch posts interesting and valuable information about free-range sites and search engines. These can be frivolous, even silly, but they do serve as a barometer of sorts. Sites such as the "Idea Directory" (at Researchpaper.com) propose topics in areas like "Society" that include drug problems and similar areas for research and add value to the topics listed via questions, statements to be supported or shredded, and other approaches that have great appeal to young writers as they suggest format and structure for the research project. National Public Radio's "Present at the Creation" takes a look at non-traditional subjects, presenting basic information about them and providing links to more sources, including multimedia. Subjects are interesting and even funny and could appeal to students. The Internet Tourbus consistently lists outstanding sites in its "Guide to the Most Useful Sites in the World." For selectors the hands down favorite web site might well be the Virtual Acquisition Shelf and Newsdesk, a wonderful blog. Although a U. K. site, it covers the information waterfront with news, reviews, and links. *Frontline* on PBS devotes its programming to issues of current interest, producing provocative programs that are intelligent additions to contemporary collections and suggest further materials that might be useful. The AllYouCanRead.com site gathers material from news media all over the planet and organizes it and provides a search function. For those inclined to try to keep up with current events, Slate compiles a daily briefing from major newspapers. These, along with educational and government sites, are among the best of the zillions of free sites out there that support this kind of research.

Publishers' lists may also reflect contemporary culture if they specialize in topical publications. For example, Prometheus Books lists a range of contemporary issues titles, as does Facts on File/Greenhaven, particularly in its Opposing Viewpoints series. ABC-CLIO has a current events/issues section that accommodates subject browsing. These and similar products can be useful to suggest topics and materials as well as possible titles to search in local catalogs.

The Gateway Library maintains an on-line list of free Internet sites to which selectors contribute. Seeking materials in support of contemporary topics often results in discovery of sites suitable for addition to on-line reference, everything from Nationalissues.com, which examines topics of current media attention, to Noodletools.com, which deals with many aspects of the research process. These sites can also identify more issues, or subsets of large ones. Gary Price's List of Lists at http://specialissues.com presents very timely updates on a variety of topics. Finding the work of the Congressional Research Service can be a bit painful, but the information and its organization make time spent worthwhile, and the topics addressed are interesting and important.

Selectors of materials to support the research needs of new students might also take a page from their colleagues in secondary schools. Freshmen were high school seniors just a few weeks earlier, and many materials useful and familiar to them in high school remain favorites in their new roles. Publications such as the Opposing Viewpoints series are held by and suitable for secondary schools as well as colleges and universities. Periodicals geared toward K-12 librarians can also be valuable resources, providing information about what is going on in schools and reviews of relevant materials. Gail Junion-Metz' monthly column in *School Library Journal* is noteworthy as she treats specific subjects in each article, occasionally including current events web sites. *SLJ* also includes timely reviews of various media. *Book Report* and *School Library Media Activities Monthly* are also useful but have much smaller readerships and distribution and may be more difficult for academic librarians to locate.

Selectors also identify products for the Libraries' list of paid databases, some of which suggest current topics to be further developed by materials' selection. For instance, *LexisNexis Current Issues Universe* features an "Issues List" of dozens of subject categories that link to documents. *ProQuest*'s Topic Finder also provides organized help for the truly desperate. One of the most valuable on-line resources is *CQ Researcher*. For many years it has been a top-notch print resource, and it has lost nothing in its translation to electronic format. It is well-organized and non-partisan, giving balanced discussions of many current issues. It is produced by a group that has been around for fifty-seven years and has set the standard for this type of research and reporting. Teaching students to use these and similar databases also provides opportunities to discuss defining topics and limiting and expanding them as well as creation of keywords and subject headings within each database, ideas usually new to beginning students.

All of these considerations are user-centered because selections of materials in this area are almost entirely defined by student interests, which change rapidly to mirror continuous developments in popular culture. Research also shows that both students and faculty members try online library materials before looking at print resources (Greenstein and Healy 2002; Jones 2002), so selectors need to check these sources often. Selectors' attention to these methods of identifying topics in contemporary living also provides an additional benefit for students. Interaction with students during class and individual instruction sessions gives librarians the opportunity to pass along to students information about selection criteria and integration of information resources and to show students the best free web sites for their work. There is also room for proselytizing the value of learning to use the library and its resources as the foundation for academic success and how to go about doing so.

Sources that feed possible research topics to selectors also identify materials in many cases, working hand in glove. In addition, keeping a traditional file of announcements of forthcoming materials identifies new resources or new formats for old favorites, such as on-line versions of traditionally print materials. Gateway may in some cases contribute acquisitions funds to those of others to enable database purchase. Other sources include review journals, publishers' materials and web sites as already mentioned, catalogs of other institutions, vendors' websites, course syllabi from this and other university web sites, commercial book vendor sites, which frequently include professional and lay reviews, and even broadcast web searches that can result in unexpected and interesting information.

Criteria for selecting titles dealing with contemporary topics are as important for this subject matter as they are for other library acquisitions. Content may be most critical. What is the scope of the work? For whom is it intended and what is its purpose? Is it accurate and up to date? Does it include bibliographies or other references that raise the level of scholarship for the reader? Is it indexed, and, if so, is the indexing accurate, well-organized, and based on useful subjects and keywords? How is the information presented? Is the order of the content intelligent? What is the level of the writing? Are biases apparent? Does it deliver its promised product? Authority is also important. Who are the authors and publisher? Is this a new work or a rehashing or a revision of an earlier one? What are the background and qualifications of the author(s)? Is expertise evident? The format of the work should be examined with quality in binding, graphics, and other physical aspects in mind. Cost is always a factor, first, in regard to the title's being worth the price being asked and, second, in its affordability. Of course, this is particularly important when selecting vendor-supplied databases. These also call into play issues of database maintenance and all the aspects of site evaluation: organization and navigation; usability, especially if graphics are a large part of the site; aesthetics; load time; help or navigation aids present and easy to use; characteristics and viability of links within the site.

Considerations of the future of contemporary topics selections are exciting. The Libraries' instructional programming group is beginning to add accessory pages to web pages available to instructors of introductory English courses, and these will include or point to some of these selections. Librarians are also beginning to add content to course management software course guides, which are becoming widely used on our campus. Our charge is to drop appropriate library resources into courses using ANGEL (A New Global Environment for Learning) CMS, which we can do independently, adding or changing content as necessary. This gives us an opportunity to connect these courses directly to the library and its resources, including the people and services not always obvious or visible to patrons not physically present in the building. On-line resources are nothing new, but new ways of presenting and integrating them are evolving rapidly. Being able to point students to basic or enriching materials empowers librarians and involves them in the teaching process in new ways. Carol A. Twigg's "Innovations in Online Learning: Moving beyond a Significant Difference" gathers together a bouquet of case studies chosen to demonstrate what can happen when educators operate outside the box, providing creative springboards to developing future programs. Innovation and inspiration will create new responsibilities and possibilities for materials' selectors because we will be thinking of using materials in ways not apparent in the past or even the present. Collaboration is key and will continue to be.

At Penn State groups of students are being targeted and presented with customized library programs through outreach efforts because they are perceived as being underserved in various ways and for various reasons. Adult learners will soon have specific pages and activities geared toward their circumstances and interests, with a real effort underway to change their actual classroom experiences in several positive ways. This effort will also target graduate students who are in fact adult learners and who often have appallingly poor research skills. The Gateway librarian is involved in developing this outreach effort, which has already resulted in adaptations in materials selection to meet their needs as courses are redesigned for them. Another underserved group of students, our student athletes, numbers around eight hundred, with dozens more engaged in club sports and intramurals. These students need specific services because they have rigid schedules, both on campus and on the road. First-year athletes often have self-contained classes, with coursework that varies from those of the rest of new students. Web pages are being developed for them to supplement the special library instruction designed for them. Other large populations include our World Campus and Study Abroad students, who come in to Libraries' resources in various ways. Services are being provided to them in nontraditional ways, and their requirements also affect selections. It is interesting to try to imagine how these and other targeted groups of students will bring new sets of considerations to the collection development table.

The actual construction of an acquisitions policy statement is facilitated to a great extent by the Libraries' outline of the criteria that should be included. Perhaps the most critical element is that these statements are intended to provide information to people who are not librarians as they are created for the Libraries Development Office. Therefore, they are not intended to be blueprints or rigid documents in any way. Indeed, they should be very flexible as they are subject to change, the only certainty in today's world. The guidelines state that they should contain:

- A description of the literature of the discipline.
- Scope of materials collected.
- Description of the existing collection.
- Description of the user community or communities.
- Strengths of the collection.
- Areas needing enhancement.
- Information regarding the appropriateness of electronic resources.
- Information concerning the benefits that the acquisition of the item could make to the field of study, researcher, or scholar.

These do not always work for Contemporary Topics, but they are useful to keep in mind, especially as one begins to learn the collection and is able to identify areas that need augmenting.

It is suggested that collection development policy statements include a wide range of informative statements. Again, some of them do not pertain to Contemporary Topics, and it is necessary to point that out in the document. Principal selectors should be named, the people responsible for this part of the collection, as this facilitates dialogue with other selectors. The primary location of the collection being discussed should be stated. This is not possible for this group of materials except for electronic selections as these materials are scattered amongst the general collection. Nor is it possible to discuss the collection itself because these selections are not identified in any way. Subject and language modifiers are not critical in this part of the collection as most materials are not limited by subject and will be available only in English.

The following document is offered as a possible collection development tool. It is the result of a rather long process of identification and attempts at setting down procedures and processes that might stand the test of time and be of use to the Libraries. It will be fun to see how it needs to be changed as times and technology change. What will the next best thing be, either in popular culture, in the ways libraries do business, or both?

GATEWAY LIBRARY
COLLECTION DEVELOPMENT POLICY
CONTEMPORARY TOPICS

General Statement

The purpose of this selection and acquisition policy statement is to provide the framework for acquiring material to support the missions of the Gateway Library in service, outreach, and information packaging as well as the general reference requirements of the University at large. It is intended to be a flexible document, subject to periodic revision to meet evolving criteria and changing times.

Programmatic Information

The Gateway Library is charged with providing entry level instruction and first-level reference assistance, which can frequently be specific to the research requirements of General Education courses, with particular attention to Rhetoric and Composition (English 015). The Gateway is all-electronic, having no print collection but being responsible for selecting current print and non-print material that will find its way among the subject libraries' collections. Gateway also contributes to the identification and selection of general reference electronic resources in support of its goals and the needs of its patrons, including the general public. "Contemporary Topics" materials may include, but not be limited to, those related to current events, contemporary issues, "hot" topics, local interest, public debate, current affairs, and other subjects that support introductory English courses and general interest requirements.

Coordination and Cooperative Information

The Gateway's "collection" is less identifiable by subject and/or location than those of the subject libraries as its focus constantly changes with current events and with topics of current interest to students beginning their academic lives. Purchases typically are dispersed among various subject libraries. Electronic selections are part of the Libraries' database collection. Selectors also work with other sections in the identification and selection of on-line resources useful to and suitable for undergraduate study. The Gateway Library also maintains links to e-reference sources, primarily those openly available on the Internet. The task of identifying topics for development generally falls to Gateway's selectors but is, on occasion, informed by other faculty as well as staff.

Subject, Time, and Language Modifiers

Subjects can be as diverse as the interests of students engaged in rhetoric, composition, and other forms of communication determine. Keywords as well as subject headings may be used to aid in the selection process. Emphasis is placed on current events and topics, although retrospective materials may be considered if renewed interest in them develops. No restrictions for retention apply. Discretion of selectors in the subject libraries actually housing them governs withdrawal of these materials, particularly if they become unusable for any reason. English language materials are selected, although database materials may be available in alternative languages.

Description of Materials Collected

Materials collected are generally in print format, and many are published just-in-time to address popular interest as events unfold in our country and the greater world and will have current publication dates. They may focus on current events or people in the news or on historical or cultural topics of return popularity. They may be available in the popular press rather than through academic publishers and vendors. Items such as the electronic version of the Encyclopedia Britannica are included as they provide background information as well as timely updates on a wide variety of topics, offering a base for further research and study. Databases such as CQ Researcher are closely reviewed by Gateway selectors as well. Books and other materials selected are dispersed throughout the Libraries' collections and may be juvenile literature, scholarly treatments, or anything in-between, depending on subject, availability, and need. Videos may also be considered, especially those such as the Frontline series. Certainly, students can satisfy some of their research needs by using periodicals and newspapers, on-line and print, and their use is encouraged, but Gateway's selections do not include these as they are provided by other means. Some selections may be seen as adding to popular culture holdings, becoming evidence of passing trends and even fads as time passes and may be viewed as commentary on historical events and the changing philosophy and sociology of our society.

Other Considerations

Many sources are consulted for collection development, including local and national newspapers' book sections, Booklist, Publishers

Weekly, and a myriad of publications and other sources, print and on-line, reporting on or detailing current topics and events. Note is also made of student requests for information as well as topics that are proposed during instruction sessions.

REFERENCES

Daniel Greenstein and Leigh Watson Healy, "Print and Electronic Information: Shedding New Light on Campus Use," EDUCAUSE review, September/October 2002, <http://www.educause.edu/pub/er/> (4 November 02).

Steve Jones, "The Internet Goes to College: How Students are Living in the Future with Today's Technology," *Pew Internet and Family Life Project*, 15 September 2002, <http://www.pewinternet.org/reports/toc.asp?Report=71> (26 September 2002).

Carol A. Twigg, "Innovations in Online Learning: Moving Beyond No Significant Difference," *Pew Learning and Technology Program*, <http://www.center.rpi.edu/PewHome.html> (26 September 2002).

APPENDIX

SELECTED FREE-RANGE INTERNET SITES

http://www.google.com
http://static.wc.ask.com/docs/about/jeevesiq.html
http://cyberatlas.internet.com/
http://info.alexa.com/
http://newslink.org/
http://www.searchenginewatch.com/
http://www.researchpaper.com/
http://www.npr.org/programs/morning/features/patc/crackerjack/index.html
http://www.tourbus.com/
http://resourceshelf.freepint.com
http://www.pbs.org/wgbh/pages/frontline/
http://www.allyoucanread.com
http://slate.msn.com/
http://www.nationalissues.com/
http://www.noodletools.com/
http://www.specialissues.com/
http://www.cnie.org/NLE/CRS/
http://www.house.gov/shays/CRS/CRSProducts.htm

Impact of Technical Services' Policies on Access and Collection Development

Magda El-Sherbini

SUMMARY. This paper will put forth some ideas about how library technical services are dealing with "the information revolution" and what impact this has on library collections and access to them. An attempt is made here to survey some of the key factors which are contributing to the gradual redefinition of access, collections and technical services. These include the changing role of technical services and cataloging departments, the impact of electronic and digital materials on library acquisitions and processing, implications of applying national cataloging standards, local cataloging practices, book vendors and the use of their records in library catalogs, remote storage decisions, and the role that library schools play in educating new generations of cataloging professionals. *[Article copies available for a fee from The Haworth Document Delivery Service: 1-800-HAWORTH. E-mail address: <docdelivery@haworthpress.com> Website: <http://www.HaworthPress.com> © 2003 by The Haworth Press, Inc. All rights reserved.]*

KEYWORDS. Technical services, cataloging, electronic publishing, book vendors, remote storage, library schools, access, collection development

Magda El-Sherbini is Associate Professor and Head of Cataloging, The Ohio Sate University Libraries, 1858 Neil Avenue Mall, Columbus, OH 43210 (E-mail: el-sherbini@osu.edu).

[Haworth co-indexing entry note]: "Impact of Technical Services' Policies on Access and Collection Development." El-Sherbini, Magda. Co-published simultaneously in *The Acquisitions Librarian* (The Haworth Information Press, an imprint of The Haworth Press, Inc.) No. 30, 2003, pp. 101-116; and: *Collection Development Policies: New Directions for Changing Collections* (ed: Daniel C. Mack) The Haworth Information Press, an imprint of The Haworth Press, Inc., 2003, pp. 101-116. Single or multiple copies of this article are available for a fee from The Haworth Document Delivery Service [1-800-HAWORTH, 9:00 a.m. - 5:00 p.m. (EST). E-mail address: docdelivery@haworthpress.com].

http://www.haworthpress.com/store/product.asp?sku=J101
© 2003 by The Haworth Press, Inc. All rights reserved.
10.1300/J101v15n30_09

INTRODUCTION

It is entirely possible that nearly every article written during the last two decades on library issues begins with a statement about the changes taking place in libraries, the publishing industry or the web and about methods of disseminating information at the end of the XXth century. The information industry is undergoing a revolution and this is reflected in professional literature devoted to it. Attempting to describe the process, while being subjected to it, is a difficult undertaking.

Along with the changes in the information industry came the need to redefine some of the fundamental concepts of library management. These changes became manifest first in the ways in which libraries came to view cataloging and library collections and how these terms became redefined. As the library community left the comfortable world of print and fiche and moved into the realm of virtual text, it faced many issues. Some of those dealt with ownership. The term "acquisition" began to include the concept of "access" and sometimes be replaced by it. Without ownership, the whole process of cataloging, classifying and processing of materials came under scrutiny. Permanence of information, methods of access, and underlying technologies providing that access came to be viewed as more important than traditional cataloging and processing.

The library community had to respond quickly to the competition coming from the Internet and the virtual information industry. Significant portions of library budgets were diverted to this digital arena, and this is having a major impact on how the library collections are defined, treated and accessed. Growing numbers of decision-makers in the library and information world maintain that paper is out and digital is in and that anything that is not current is not that relevant. Such one-sided tendencies have major implications for access.

This paper will put forth some ideas about how library technical services are dealing with "the information revolution" and what impact this has on library collections and access to them. An attempt is made here to survey some of the key factors which are contributing to the gradual redefinition of access, collections and technical services. These include the changing role of technical services and cataloging departments, the impact of electronic and digital materials on library acquisitions and processing, implications of applying national cataloging standards, local cataloging practices, book vendors and the use of their records in library catalogs, remote storage decisions, and the role that library schools play in educating new generations of cataloging professionals.

TECHNICAL SERVICES
AND CATALOGING DEPARTMENTS

Throughout the 1990s, many libraries came under continued financial pressure which had its origins in a variety of factors that impacted all aspects of the information industry. Rising costs of scientific publications, emergence of electronic publishing and high costs of providing adequate bibliographic access are just a few.

In the area of library technical services, budget limitations forced libraries to review their organizational structures and their policies governing library acquisition of materials as well as cataloging and processing of materials. Placed under financial constraints, library administrators looked for cost-saving techniques and tended to find them in their cataloging departments. According to Dorner "budget freezes or reductions and escalating costs have been part and parcel of library administration for the past two decades, and in most libraries, cataloging has borne much of brunt."[1]

In making decisions to limit the amount of resources in technical services in general and cataloging departments in particular, library administrators tended to scrutinize the overall cost of processing of materials in libraries and base their decisions on these factors. Studies conducted at the time revealed that the cost of processing materials was excessively high. It was perceived that relatively low productivity of professional catalogers contributed to those statistics. As the pressure to cut costs and expedite processing continued to grow, experienced, long-term catalogers bore much of the blame for libraries' inability to cope with the demands of the changing information world and make quick decisions. Catalogers were charged with lacking imagination and resisting change. In his work on this subject Waite mentioned that "technical service organizations, especially our catalog department, have three features that do not mesh well with the new environment: they are expensive, they are slow, and they do not meet the information expectations for our customers."[2]

Growing demands for greater access to materials and growing budget limitations coupled with the deteriorating image of catalogers, the high cost of cataloging, and the low productivity forced many administrators to rethink cataloging and their cataloging departments.

While cataloging and cataloging departments appeared to be in trouble and were not favored by library administrators, collections and collection development continued to grow as libraries acquired materials almost on the same pace as before. The budget cut or freeze did not have a proportionate effect on collection development and generally did not place restrictions on what libraries might buy. Although serials acquisition was somewhat curtailed, many new formats, including electronic, soon filled that void.

Significant reductions in cataloging units coupled with pressure to keep pace with the demand for access to materials forced libraries to shift their policymaking and to look for solutions outside the library. One type of solution was found with vendor service providers who were eager to enter the marketplace and provide services for what constituted one of the core responsibilities of the library. Statistical surveys show that some academic libraries indicate that many vendors are being used for outsourcing of all or parts of their cataloging.[3] Some libraries, such as Wright State University, eliminated their cataloging departments and outsourced the entire cataloging to OCLC TECHPRO.[4] Other libraries re-engineered cataloging by using staff (non-MLS employees) to do cataloging. Other libraries took a different approach and applied streamlining and modifying the workflow to simplify and speed up the processing of their materials.

Ohio State University Libraries provide a good example of a library that faced these challenges by applying multiple approaches. The current Cataloging Department is not as comprehensive as it once was. During the last seven years the role of the department was redefined. For example, cataloging is currently being done successfully by non-professional staff and graduate students.[5] Cataloging functions have been dispersed among several departments. For example, simple copy cataloging for English language materials is done in the Acquisitions Department (currently Monograph Department) and it is performed upon receipt. In addition, outsourcing was introduced and implemented successfully when the library lost several expert foreign language materials catalogers due to budget cuts.[6] Cataloging had also implemented the PromptCat services to obtain cataloging records directly from a vendor.[7] This multi-faceted approach allowed the library to deal with the budget crunch and continue providing access to most materials coming into the library.

All these changes had a major impact on the technical services training policy. Technical services had to change their training policy to meet the needs of the non-professional staff and graduate students who were now doing much of the cataloging. Special training had to be designed that would provide a combination of theory of cataloging as well as practice. Training also had to be focused on individual assignments to assure quality and understanding of the principles of cataloging. In some cases, cross training among high-level staff was necessary, especially when the library had limited staff.

Furthermore, the catalogers' role in the library changed from simply performing cataloging to "(1) providing leadership for bibliographic control activities in the library as well as in the profession, (2) creating the bibliographic access system for the library, (3) coordinating bibliographic access policies, (4) training, (5) managing a bibliographic access department or system, (6) innovating, (7) boundary-spanning, (8) evaluating the performance of the bibliographic access department or system, and (9) interpreting and conducting research."[8]

The role of technical service librarians is changing as they engage in mediation and become liaisons, communicating local cataloging and processing policies to their colleagues in the public service departments. Information brokers at the reference desk need to know how the mixed sources of cataloging impact access and what they are losing or gaining by these mixed sources of records. For example, when a library contracts all or part of cataloging to an external vendor, cataloging is done on the basis of specifications that are provided to the vendor. These specifications take into account contracting and workflow processes. Patrons' needs are usually taken into account when contracts are drawn up, but they tend not to be in the forefront of these considerations.

All of these changes in cataloging processes have a profound effect on access. With the lack of experienced in-house catalogers, much of cataloging is now delegated to non-professional catalogers, including students, or is being outsourced to external cataloging vendors. Results obtained from such mixed sources are not always reliable and contribute to the overall problem of record quality and access.

ELECTRONIC AND DIGITAL MATERIALS AND THEIR IMPACT ON ACQUISITIONS BUDGETS

Substantial changes taking place in academic and research libraries in the 1990s included budget reductions, spiraling costs of materials, introduction of new information and communication technologies and a general explosion of digital information. In order to respond to the information needs of their users and to keep pace with technological development in the information industry, libraries began to embrace the concept of the digital library. In broad terms, it means moving toward the concept of providing access to and bibliographic description for digital materials that the library may or may not own.

Initially, this meant investing in technical infrastructure and creating modest acquisitions budgets for digital materials. As this trend continued libraries were faced with the need to look at their operations and organizational structures. Changes in information availability and communication flows favored a trend to reorganize in an effort to meet the needs of the new, technologically savvy generation of library users in many instances, reorganization tended to favor a flattening of organizational structures.

Creating a virtual library and diverting significant parts of the materials budget to electronic resources had a profound impact on technical service organizations in general and cataloging departments in particular. Many cataloging units organized along traditional lines seemed unable to address the challenge of cataloging and processing of digital information. Grenci in her article discussed in detail the impact of web publishing on the organization of cataloging functions. In her study, she pointed out that "institutions that organize their cataloging function according to one of the traditional models are finding themselves increasingly unable to meet the demands being placed upon the new environment. Traditional models of organization can, and must be modified to successfully deal with this problem."[9]

Libraries responded to this situation in a variety of ways. To meet the challenge of electronic publishing and digitization, some cataloging departments' functions were integrated with other technical service departments and new departments were formed. One of the models, applied at the Ohio State University Libraries, merged the Serials Section in the Cataloging Department with the Serials Acquisitions to form a new Serials and Electronic Resources Department. Other strategies would divert staff from departments that processed print materials to departments or units processing digital materials. This move could be easily implemented when positions became vacant. In one such example when the position of Coordinator of Western Languages Cataloging Section in the Cataloging Department became vacant, it was moved to the Serials and Electronic Resources Department to accommodate the workload increase in this area.

While this type of reorganization tended to favor the high profile digital collection processing it did not take into account the impact it would have on access to print materials. Traditional cataloging units continued to lose positions while their cataloging stream did not decrease.

As libraries focused their energies on addressing the needs of the digital information community, emphasis on processing of print materials along traditional models began to wane. Library administrators began to seek other alternatives, in part at least to compensate for this gap. Internal solutions involved using para-professional staff to do cataloging previously done by professional catalogers. In academic institutions, it often involved hiring part-time student assistants to perform these functions. Outsourcing of the work became a viable option as outside vendors began to offer ready cataloging records for new materials, or offer contract cataloging services.

Regardless of the impact of electronic resources and acquiring digital formats on cataloging or technical service organization, these materials need to be cataloged and made available to patrons. Cataloging them is not a miracle. Cataloging departments faced the challenge of providing access to materials in different formats for many years. Electronic resources should not be treated any differently then other formats and should not constitute a threat to functioning technical service units in most libraries.

The rules for cataloging apply equally to print and electronic formats. The decision to catalog them as a single record or multiple records is already clear and gives libraries much flexibility to apply these rules. The real challenge facing technical services is to make the selection policy for electronic resources coherent and clear and to articulate that the library does not have the responsibility to buy and catalog everything that is available on the web.

Many libraries today focus their attention on cataloging electronic resources, web sites, and virtual information sources. Shifts in materials budgets and reallocation of staff testify to this trend. This change of focus has a direct impact on purchasing and processing of printed materials. Although there is no evidence to suggest that there is a decrease in buying printed materials, there is substantial evidence of the tremendous increase in buying of digital materials.

THE IMPACT OF APPLYING NATIONAL CATALOGING STANDARDS ON ACCESS

Library literature has already addressed the importance of applying national cataloging standards and there are no arguments about the benefits of these standards. Organization of information according to Dewey or MARC is the backbone of library and information industry. Catalogers have been applying and will continue to apply these standards as they provide the users with access to the full range of research materials in all formats. They built a strong knowledge base and expertise in using AACR2, Library of Congress Rule Interpretations, Library of Congress Subject Headings, LC Subject Cataloging Manual, Library of Congress Classification, and the MARC (machine-readable cataloging) format for bibliographic data.

Applying national cataloging standards has a great impact on collection development and its use. Through national cataloging standards, libraries and bibliographic utilities (such as OCLC WorldCat and RLIN) are able to transmit knowledge about what information is held where, what subjects are covered, how much material is held in a collection, whether there are restrictions on use, origin of the records, and other physical and intellectual characteristics of the original source material.

What is new in the current discussion of standards is related to the newborn cataloging standards. The advent of electronic publishing gave rise to a proliferation of standards that are being applied to process and catalog information. OCLC Connexion, for example, is now providing bibliographic records in MARC and Dublin Core standards.[10] Both the user and the cataloger will definitely feel the impact of these changes. Today's catalogers are faced with a proliferation of new cataloging standards and have the choice and the flexibility to apply standards that are appropriate for each format.

As the new standards are being applied, technical service policies regarding cataloging have to be changed to reflect these new coming standards and to explain and educate their users, including acquisitions and reference librarians, on the use of these standards.

Multiple standards are not the only issues that have an effect on access. Change in the current standards and revised rules, such as AACR2 revised, MARC, LCSH, etc., also have an impact on maintaining consistency in the online databases and in access to information. Catalogers and information users need to be educated about the application of the new concepts of catalog records and how to deal with the new approaches to cataloging, especially for web and electronic resources.

Many library administrations tend to view the role of cataloging and applying national standards as diminishing in libraries. This approach is somewhat one-sided and not adequate to meet the information needs of tomorrow. Libraries need to invest not only in the acquisition of material, but also in the description and organization of those resources in shared formats. The Library of Congress' Program for Cooperative Cataloging (PCC) is one of the most successful programs for cataloging. It is an international cooperative effort aimed at expanding access to library collections by "providing useful, timely and cost-effective cataloging that meets mutually accepted standards of libraries around the world."[11] The PCC has four components: NACO (The name authority program), SACO (the subject authority program), BIBCO (the monographic bibliographic record program), and CONSER (the cooperative online series program).

By participating in this program, libraries will not only have access to local bibliographic records but also will increase the sharing and use of foreign bibliographic and authority records. This in particular will have a positive impact on acquisitions in general and acquiring foreign language materials in particular.

There are many discussions about whether to incorporate the cataloging of library web pages and Internet resources in the library catalog. Some libraries prefer to have a comprehensive catalog rather than having separate universes for traditional library resources and Internet resources. Authority control, subject access, and other cataloging standards should be applied to these resources.[12]

APPLYING LOCAL CATALOGING PRACTICES AND ITS IMPACT ON COLLECTIONS

Many libraries apply local cataloging practices to describe certain collections or to shelflist materials in an alphabetical order, or to group materials by subject. Results of the decision to implement local practices have a great impact on access to collections and on collection development. At times, local practice decisions conflict with LC classification, making access to parts of collections difficult.

The Ohio State University Libraries have a long-standing tradition of applying local cataloging practices for shelflisting purposes. These local-cataloging practices have undergone numerous changes in the past ten years. Among these was the decision to eliminate paper shelflisting in the early 90s and to discontinue shelflisting for all classes except classes M, N, and Ps.[13] At the same time, many other local practices have been applied to call numbers. These cataloging local practices are: adjusting call number for Classes M, N, and Ps; revised literature table 40 of class P; three (or more) cutters; OSU cuttering tables; OSU translation tables; adaptations, criticisms, etc.; editions and conferences; class "Z" for bibliographies; prefixes and suffixes in call numbers.

There are two main reasons why OSU Libraries don't always follow LC:

- Local practice has been followed at OSUL for many years (e.g., Z8 for biography) and a number of records/books already exist with that number;
- Collection managers have requested a change in procedures (e.g., subject bibliographies in the subject classification number instead of in "Z" class).

These local cataloging practices are now under review and a decision needs to be made whether OSUL should continue using them. There are clear advantages to eliminating cataloging local practices, consistency of cataloging being but one. At the same time however, eliminating local practice will have an impact on the traditional ways of accessing and using the collection.

1. Application of cataloging local practice allowed the library to maintain detailed information on what it owns, in what subject areas, and in what languages or by author. This was an advantage in the past when the online catalog was not available and users as well as collection mangers depended on open stacks to browse the collection and easily recognize the strength of the collection. With the elimination of local practice, the ability to browse the stacks by call number is limited. An argument can be made that with the advent of the online catalog and its capabilities, collection managers and users are now able to browse the collection through their OPAC and obtain this information electronically.
2. Elimination of local practice will produce inconsistencies in the call number assignments and in shelving materials in the stacks. This problem already exists, because of the history of shelflisting.
3. Applying local practice has proven to be expensive. Every record has to be checked against the shelflist and the call number had to be changed or modified to agree with the shelflist. This practice slows down the work and productivity.
4. Elimination of local practice will help reduce the cost of cataloging.
5. Elimination of local practice will allow member libraries to use each other's records in the OCLC database more effectively, (without making major changes) since all cataloging will conform to national standards.
6. Eliminating local cataloging practice will also allow the library to look at all the options available for providing bibliographic records, such as vendor record and shelf ready materials.

VENDOR SERVICES
AND THEIR IMPACT ON CATALOG RECORDS

In the late 90s, OCLC and RLIN began to add to their database records created by foreign booksellers. This practice was accepted by libraries as a feasible alternative to cataloging in-house, but questions about the quality of records obtained from vendors became an issue. In his article on vendor records, Beall pointed out the impact of vendor records on cataloging and access in academic libraries. He mentioned in his analysis that "vendor records tend to be of very low bibliographic quality. They do not follow minimal-level cataloging and generally do not have authorized forms for names, series, and subject headings."[14]

Questions regarding the quality of cataloging led academic libraries to direct their attention to vendor records and closely examine them. At OSUL, records from Harrasowitz are reviewed by catalogers and in most case are enhanced locally before they are added to the on-line catalog. Failure to follow such procedures could have posed a threat to the usability of the online catalog in the future. Since cataloging is done at OSUL by non-MLS catalogers, this work requires a great deal of time and in some cases slows down the workflow. Diverting resources to this process has a negative impact on original cataloging in that these materials are not processed upon receipt and as a result, they are not made available to patrons in a timely fashion.

Outsourcing can be an acceptable alternative to in-house cataloging, but it is fair to say that some catalog records obtained from vendors will not have the level of detail or accuracy that an in-house cataloger can provide. In-house catalogers have a combination of experience and much needed contact with the user. They can very easily identify what the users needs are and what kind of access they will look for. In addition, there is no limitation or restriction on how many fields need to be included in the bibliographic records. In contract cataloging the contractee has to set up a limit on how many subject headings will be in the bibliographic record, while in-house catalogers will add as many subject headings as are necessary to describe the content of materials.

REMOTE LIBRARY STORAGE

Many large academic and research libraries are using remote storage facilities to meet the need for shelving space created by the constant growth in library materials. Although remote storage has always been part of the solution to the problem of space in libraries, it seems to be more of a factor now, when so much emphasis in libraries is placed on instant access to materials. Why, then, is this becoming such a dilemma for libraries today? Are library materials budgets getting better? Is the cost of publishing decreasing? Regardless of the answer, moving selected materials to remote storage facilities is a fact of life for many libraries.

In his article on this topic, Seeds discussed some methods of de-selecting materials to be transferred to remote storage. He mentioned a number of factors which were considered in the de-selection process. These factors included duplicate materials, low usage, low circulation counts for monographs, amount of dust on materials, age of materials, foreign languages, poor condition, ceased and cancelled serial titles.[15]

Transferring of library materials to storage facilities has a great impact on access. One of the negative impacts on access is that the users of information can no longer walk into open stacks and browse the library collection. In addition, users sometimes have to wait for a long time for materials to arrive from storage. This in particular creates inconvenience to users and information seekers. Furthermore, the library collection is divided into the in-house collection and the off-site collection. This division makes it impossible for collection managers to scan the stacks to get a sense of what is in the collection.[16]

Housing some parts of the collection in remote storage facilities creates an unanticipated problem for the library administrator. As the volume of materials sent to storage increases, so does the need to provide better information in the bibliographic record. In order to guarantee good access to materials stored off-site, a full cataloging record has to be produced for those materials. Such a record might require the table of contents (TOC), more access points, such as additional authors, part of the title, and many subject headings. These enhancements help to provide valuable information for the item being stored remotely, making it accessible through the on-line catalog. This means allocating more resources to cataloging and increasing the number of qualified catalogers. This may be difficult to achieve at a time when library administrators are cutting back on cataloging and cataloger positions.

An argument could be made that the cause of these problems is the lack of a healthy collection development policy approach that is based on patrons needs. As Carrigan pointed out, "The collection development is responsible for making-up of the collections. The better job done matching the collections with the needs and interests of patrons, the greater will be the use of the collections, the attendant benefit, and thus the return on the investment in the collection."[17]

LIBRARY SCHOOL'S IMPACT ON TECHNICAL SERVICES

Library schools have always played a vital role in educating new generations of librarians who needed the knowledge of cataloging and classification theory and practice. As these professionals entered the work place, they benefited from the vast experience of senior catalogers who imparted their knowledge to the younger generation. This seemingly permanent symbiosis seems to be threatened by two trends that appear to be occurring simultaneously. The first is the continuous depletion of the ranks of senior experienced catalogers in libraries. The other is the flight of library school students from traditional cataloging courses in favor of technology driven curriculum.

Library technical service divisions in general and cataloging departments in particular are losing many experienced catalogers and technical staff as an entire generation of librarians considers retirement or leaves the profession. These positions are rarely, if ever, filled with staff of equal experience and expertise. Important cataloging knowledge is lost in the process as there is little opportunity to pass it on to the new generation. A recent email message indicated that the Cataloging Directorate of Library Services had lost 205 FTEs since 1990 and as a result they can no longer afford to perform quality cataloging because of insufficient professional staff. This situation has negative impact on the quality of cataloging. As a result, acquisitions and reference staff cannot adequately perform their duties when they can no longer rely on the accuracy of cataloging records.[18]

Library schools have a great role to play in the era of information processing. They always focused their attention on teaching curriculum to support the traditional functions of the libraries, such as management, technical services and public services. In teaching cataloging, library schools stressed the importance of the cataloging tools that were used in libraries to organize print and film collections.

Now, library schools are also supporting the fast development in technology and are devising ways in which the new librarian can meet the challenge provided by the diversity of the information industry. Schools have to develop courses that will impart the knowledge necessary in organizing information to meet today's information needs. In her presentation at the American Library Association Congress on Professional Education, Bates addressed the issue of the new challenges of processing digital formats when she said, "When it comes to cataloging, we need to prepare professionals who can recognize generic information description problems and translate them across all media. The AACR2 and Library of Congress Subject Headings will not do for all information in all environments. Our students need to be able to select an indexing language for a website's database, or develop an electronic finding list for an online archival collection."[19]

Catalogers and cataloging departments were the backbone of the library operations because of the important role they played in organizing information. In the early 1990s, catalogers began to experience tension brought about by the changes in their responsibility and felt that the important role they played in the past is diminishing. They also felt more pressure from the library administrators because of the nature of their detailed work. These developments eventually effected library schools and the role of cataloging in the curriculum. It seems that many students are no longer interested in cataloging jobs or cataloging courses because of the criticism that catalogers are facing. In addition, some library schools were no longer teaching cataloging and as Beacom said, ". . . we have counterexamples of good schools closing altogether."[20]

As Turitz mentioned in his response to an email message related to teaching of cataloging, "Cataloging should be a requirement for graduation from library school (or information science as it is now often called). Even though the numbers of catalogers has gone down as more of it is outsourced and library schools no longer have cataloging as a requirement, we still need professionals who understand what decisions need to be made about the online catalog and what quality of cataloging/authority control. Etc."[21]

Library schools and library technical service units have a dual and complementary role to play in today's library. Beacom mentioned that "If library schools do not prepare students to add value to services and products in a networked information environment, then librarians–meaning "graduates of library schools"–will not be a part of scholarly communication."[22] And if technical services will not promote catalogers and redefine the role of catalogers in organizing information, the library profession will no longer have control over this function.

CONCLUSION

For some time now, library administrators are under significant pressure to reduce their costs and improve access to library materials. In attempting to deal with budget limitations, many look to cataloging departments to reduce their cost of operation. Having reduced their staff and with growing demands to catalog materials, they turned to third parties to help them provide access. Outsourcing services began to flourish, but the question of quality of their records and its impact on access remains unanswered.

All the while there is great pressure to produce high quality, expensive cataloging records. Libraries are committed to complex national cataloging standards, and ever changing local practices. They often have to contend with large parts of their collections being stored in remote locations and not easily accessible to users. Library policies are being changed to accommodate the need to provide access to the Internet and digital materials. As libraries overextend themselves to attain these goals, they continue to reduce their cataloging functions.

Technical service policies also play an important role in the cataloging function as a whole, as they impact the cataloger's job market tremendously. Elimination of cataloger's positions in libraries has lowered the total number of catalogers active in the profession. Many entry level (MLS) librarians with potential interest in cataloging are turning away from this option and shift their interest to public services positions as cataloging is perceived to be an unattractive and besieged part of the library organization. It is imperative for library technical services to take responsibility for redefining cataloging in light of the changes in the information processing industry. New job descriptions for catalogers have to meet today's needs and to attract new graduates, who are interested in organizing information and creating full-scale digital libraries. This will be possible if, as Beacom said ". . . they will only if library schools offer the right preparation: one that builds a foundation for growth in traditional library skills and the skills needed for the networked information environment."[23]

Finally, library administrators would do well to take another look at cataloging of library materials and come to terms with the fact that not every bit of cataloging is well served by alternative cataloging solutions. Cataloging today is becoming more complicated and requires enhanced professional skills to insure quality and accuracy in order for the users of tomorrow to get better access to library materials. Libraries also need to focus their attention on training a new generation of catalogers and provide them with new skills necessary to process materials according to national standards.

REFERENCES

1. Dorner, Dan. Cataloging in the 21st Century, Part 1: Contextual Issues. Library Collections & Technical Services. Vol. 23, No. 4, 1999. Pp. 393-399.

2. Waite, Ellen J. Reinvent Catalogers! Library Journal. Vol. 120. (Nov. 1 1995). Pp. 36-7.

3. The Impact of Outsourcing and Privatization on Library Services and Management, http://www.ala.org/alaorg/ors/outsourcing/outsourcing_toc.html.

4. Hirshon, Arnold and Winters, Barbara. Outsourcing Library Technical Services: a How-To-Do It Manual For Librarians. New York, Neal-Schuman Publishers, Inc, 1996. 172 p.

5. El-Sherbini, Magda and Klim, George. Changes in Technical Services and Their Effect on the Role of Catalogers and Staff Education: An Overview. Cataloging & Classification Quarterly. Vol. 24, No. 1/2. 1997. Pp. 23-33.

6. El-Sherbini, Magda. Contract Cataloging: a Pilot Project for Outsourcing Slavic Books. Cataloging & Classification Quarterly Vol. 20, No. 3. 1995. Pp. 57-73.

7. Rider, Mary M. PromptCat: A Projected Service for Automatic Cataloging–Results of a Study at the Ohio University Libraries. Cataloging & Classification Quarterly. Vol. 20, No. 4. 1995. Pp. 23-44.

8. Younger, Jennifer A. The Role of Librarians in Bibliographic Access Services in the 1990s. Journal of Library Administration. Vol. 15, No. 1/2. 1991. Pp.125-50.

9. Grenci, Mary. The Impact of Web Publishing on the Organization of Cataloging Functions. Library Collections, Acquisitions, and Technical Services. Vol. 24, Issue 2, summer, 2000. Pp. 153-170.

10. OCLC Connexion Web Page, http://www.oclc.org/connexion/.

11. Library of Congress. Program for Cooperative cataloging (PCC) web page, http://www.loc.gov/catdir/pcc/2001pcc.html.

12. University of California: System Wide Operations and Planning Advisory Committee (SOPAG). Electronic Resources Cataloging Task Force. 1998, http://tpot.ucsd.edu/Cataloging/HotsElectronic/SOPAG/intro.htm.

13. El-Sherbini, Magda and Stalker John C. A Study of Cutter Number Adjustment at the Ohio State University Libraries. Library Resources & Technical Services. Vol. 40, No. 4, October 1996. Pp. 319-326.

14. Beall, Jeffrey. The Impact of Vendor Records on Cataloging and Access in Academic Libraries. Library Collections, Acquisitions, and Technical Services. Vol. 24, Issue 2, summer, 2000. Pp. 229-237.

15. Seeds, Robert S. Impact of Remote Library Storage on Information Consumers: "Sophie's Choice"? Collection Building. Vol. 19, No. 3. 2000. Pp. 105-108.

16. Ibid.

17. Carrigan, Dennis P. Toward a Theory of Collection Development. Library Acquisitions: Practice & Theory. Vol. 19, No. 1. 1995. Pp. 97-106.

18. Statement of the Library of Congress Professional Guild, AFSCME Local 2910 Before the Committee on Appropriations Sub-Committee on Legislative Branch, Appropriation U.S House of Representatives. May 1, 2002, http://web.library.uiuc.edu/ahx/ead/ala/9701040a/berman/biblinks/loc.pdf.

19. Bates, Marcia J. Information Curriculum for the 21st Century. Revised as Presented to the American Library Association Congress on Professional Education. Washington, DC, May 1, 1999, http://www.ala.org/congress/bates.html.

20. Beacom, Matthew. The Catalog Librarian in the Age of the Smart Machine. A Presentation Given in 31 March 1996 at the Conference Finding Common Ground sponsored by the Harvard College Library. Cambridge, Massachusetts, http://www.library.yale.edu/~mbeacom./newbreed.htm.

21. Turitz, Mitch. Teaching Cataloging–One More Question. Online posting. 11 May 2000, http://innopacusers.org/list/archives/2000/msg01857.html.

22. Beacom, Matthew. The Catalog Librarian in the Age of the Smart Machine. A Presentation Given in 31 March 1996 at the Conference Finding Common Ground sponsored by the Harvard College Library. Cambridge, Massachusetts, http://www.library.yale.edu/~mbeacom./newbreed.htm.

23. Ibid.

Nicholson Baker Wasn't All Wrong:
A Collection Development Policy
for Remote Storage Facilities

Elka Tenner Shlomo

SUMMARY. An increasing number of libraries are engaged in building remote storage facilities. Overcrowded shelves resulting from an increase in scholarly publishing and the high cost of traditional library buildings have made remote storage attractive options. It has the further advantage of offering an environment more suited to preservation and security. However, remote storage is not a popular choice, especially among the faculty. A collection development policy is essential for these branch libraries. Librarians must involve faculty in developing the guidelines to be used in selecting materials for storage. Both general and specific criteria need to be determined so as to cause the least disruption to research and curricular needs. *[Article copies available for a fee from The Haworth Document Delivery Service: 1-800-HAWORTH. E-mail address: <docdelivery@haworthpress.com> Website: <http://www.HaworthPress.com> © 2003 by The Haworth Press, Inc. All rights reserved.]*

KEYWORDS. Collection development policies, remote storage facilities, collection maintenance, library space

Elka Tenner Shlomo is Collection Development Coordinator, Fondren Library, Rice University, Houston, TX 77251-1892 (E-mail: eshlomo@sparta.rice.edu).

[Haworth co-indexing entry note]: "Nicholson Baker Wasn't All Wrong: A Collection Development Policy for Remote Storage Facilities." Shlomo, Elka Tenner. Co-published simultaneously in *The Acquisitions Librarian* (The Haworth Information Press, an imprint of The Haworth Press, Inc.) No. 30, 2003, pp. 117-130; and: *Collection Development Policies: New Directions for Changing Collections* (ed: Daniel C. Mack) The Haworth Information Press, an imprint of The Haworth Press, Inc., 2003, pp. 117-130. Single or multiple copies of this article are available for a fee from The Haworth Document Delivery Service [1-800-HAWORTH, 9:00 a.m. - 5:00 p.m. (EST). E-mail address: docdelivery@haworthpress.com].

http://www.haworthpress.com/store/product.asp?sku=J101
© 2003 by The Haworth Press, Inc. All rights reserved.
10.1300/J101v15n30_10

INTRODUCTION

In his work *Double Fold,* Nicholson Baker[1] made himself famous (or infamous depending on your point of view) by decrying the loss of material through the weeding or preservation processes practiced in most libraries. He argues that loss of the item itself, even if rendered in a different format, prevents readers from exploring the artifactual as well as contextual value of the work. However, as most academic libraries are well aware, weeding is a necessity. Weeding allows the removal of outdated material or material no longer relevant to the curricular and research needs of its primary clientele so that new acquisitions can be comfortably accommodated.

Weeding, however, is an insufficient solution to the overcrowding that has become endemic in research libraries. With the pace of research multiplying, not only the number of resources but also the growth in pagination of serial volumes has increased dramatically. In addition to the overcrowding, thousands of books published on acidic paper are deteriorating on the shelves and need a controlled climate not possible or too costly to achieve in current library buildings. Baker cites remote storage as the best option for preservation and overcrowding when discussing the Library of Congress' ill-fated experimentation with DEZ

> With all the money the library spent noodling with fire in a vacuum . . . they could have put up several large, unflashy, dimly lit, air-conditioned print-shelters . . . that would have kept millions of low-use books, newspapers, and bound periodicals . . . awaiting their infrequent summons.[2]

BRIEF HISTORY OF REMOTE STORAGE

That libraries have turned to storage facilities to relieve overcrowding on their shelves is not new. Even the famed Library of Alexandria established a separate storage facility.[3] Academic libraries in the United States began to look at remote storage in the early 1900s as remote storage provides a vastly less expensive alternative to traditional library buildings.[4] In fact, Yale University estimates their costs to be one-tenth the cost of an open stack library on campus.[5] The New England Depository (1942) and the Midwest Inter-Library Center (1949), later to become the Center for Research Libraries in 1969, are examples of storage facilities that helped usher in remote storage in American universities since the mid Twentieth century.[6]

It was not until 1986, however, that a building designed specifically as a library storage facility was constructed for the first time by Harvard University. The Harvard Depository exhibited what are the hallmarks of remote storage facilities today–an industrial type building whose modular design allows easy expansion, shelving by size instead of call number to improve capacity, high bay adjustable shelving, use of an inventory control system for tracking, and environmental controls.[7] Brown University, Indiana University, University of Texas at Austin, Ohio State and others have followed this model when building their own facilities. ARL defines remote storage as having 50,000 items or more in a location remote from the main institution.[8]

THE BAD, THE UGLY, AND THE GOOD OF REMOTE STORAGE

Remote storage remains an unpopular choice for solving the overcrowding issue. Thought there seems to be general agreement as to what to put into a storage facility–low-use material that the library wishes to permanently retain, there is a lack of agreement on how best to predict what materials will be used. A number of studies have been conducted about the patterns of use in academic libraries. Ash,[9] Fussler and Simon,[10] and Kent et al.[11] provide in-depth examples of methodologies used to examine usage patterns. Richard W. Trueswell, an advocate of the core collection concept, has published a number of works testing his assumption that only a small percentage of the collection circulates.[12] Slote has shown "shelf-time" to be a better criterion than imprint date for predicting future use.[13] Other studies have tested the "Slote Method" and drawn similar conclusions.[14] Thus, circulation statistics are a valid means to discover what materials are being used and therefore what materials could go to storage. However, it is an imperfect method and calls for librarians to have clairvoyance as new course offerings, literary prizes, and new discoveries may peak interest in a work that never circulated previously.[15]

The faculty tendency to resist storage stems from a variety of reasons. They are concerned about the possible negative impact on research as a result of the loss of immediate access and lack of a browsing capability–the "serendipity" factor–inherent in remote storage.[16] It requires the faculty to change in their research habits and complete a request form. At least one study on the use of serials in storage has shown a decline in usage, even if there was a willingness to fill out a form, concluding storage " . . . can be a significant disincentive to patrons' use of serials."[17] The faculty may worry that titles sent to storage may never return to the active collection or will eventually be discarded altogether. Further, it has been argued that those materials selected for storage are exactly the type of resources that give a collection its unique character.[18] Selection therefore is not easy and may vary considerably from library to library depending on local circumstances and even among various branch libraries on the same campus.

Consequently, it is imperative that the librarians determine the guidelines for storage, both general and discipline specific, with the aid or approval of the faculty.[19] Institutional support, from the university administration as well as the faculty, is absolutely necessary as "Political awareness, communication, and consensus building are crucial [for success]."[20] Libraries that have an active liaison program with the faculty, in which collection development by department or program is the responsibility of reference or dedicated collection development librarians, should be able to elicit faculty reaction and make adjustments accordingly. At Rice University, several "trial balloons" were launched to determine cut-off dates for serial runs and other topics likely to be controversial. The collection development librarians contacted various individuals in their departments to seek their reaction and consul. Thus, when the Committee for Collections presented its guidelines to the Faculty Library Committee, they were approved with only slight amendments.

It should be noted that the disadvantages of storage can be somewhat ameliorated by full bibliographic description of the titles stored. Many collection development policies require an item to be fully cataloged and searchable via the library's OPAC before it can be considered for storage. Rapid delivery of items requested from storage is another key element to success and should be mentioned in the policy.[21] A reading room in the storage facility to accommodate researchers on site further serves to allay resistance to storage. While the library does not want to encourage patrons to go to the facility, in some cases it is best for the patron to examine materials on site. The policy should include information about making arrangements in advance.

THE RATIONALE FOR A COLLECTION DEVELOPMENT POLICY FOR REMOTE STORAGE

Storage facilities are essentially a branch library and therefore a collection development policy must be established. Though in many ways selecting for storage is similar to a weeding project, the scale and scope of a storage project is much larger.[22] Preservation and security are additional factors influencing decision-making for storage that do not need to be considered for weeding projects. Storage, however, should not be substituted for weeding, as it undermines the principal that the librarians are organized and employing reasoned judgment.[23]

> Ideal selection priorities will enable and also reflect a simple, expedient, reversible, and cost-effective process that takes into account considerations of collection integrity and of security and preservation.[24]

Before any storage program is implemented there must be a clear goal for the project. Thus the collection development policy for the storage facility must outline the intended purpose and criteria by which the materials are selected and most importantly, the policy must state that materials in storage may be re-evaluated for return to the active collection. The collection development policy should translate " . . . the mission and goals of the institution and the needs of its constituents into a set of long range collection goals and objectives."[25] It provides a rationale for decision-making, preserves institutional memory, ensures consistency over the years, and may help deflect faculty charges of bias in the selection process.[26]

Several works are available to assist in the evaluation of library collections and selection of materials for storage. The American Library Association has published two especially helpful guides as part of their series Collection Development and Management Guides, *Guide To Review of Library Collections: Preservation, Storage, and Withdrawal*[27] and *Guide to the Evaluation of Library Collections.*[28] Both publications provide excellent bibliographies, listed by category, for further reading. Further, Stanley J. Slote's *Weeding Library Collections: Library Weeding Methods*[29] provides an overview of the literature of weeding as well as describing a number of practical methods by which this can be accomplished.

GENERAL CRITERIA FOR STORAGE

Each academic discipline will have unique requirements that will dictate the amount and kind of material removed. The sciences generally rely most heavily on journals and currency is usually of prime concern, though this is less true of mathematics.[30] The Humanities are more dependent on monographs. They make the case that the library is their laboratory and that material published earlier may be just as valid and current as this month's journal issue. Consequently, Harvard University is keeping all Humanities print serials active from 1930.[31]

Additionally, serial publications will pose different problems than monographs and therefore different selection criteria. The library will have to decide what a serial is in this context, generally based on publication schedule. For example, are annual publications serials? Are all annual publications, such as member directories, reports, statistics, equal in their importance?[32] Establishing a cut-off date for serial runs does allow a large number of shelves to be cleared rather quickly but may provoke the largest variance in cut-off dates since the reliance on journals varies greatly from discipline to discipline. Margaret Powell relates how the faculty at Yale made suggestions for storage that significantly increased the years of serial runs to be stored, underscoring once again the importance of discipline specific criteria developed by subject specialists in collaboration with the faculty.[33]

The amount of volumes needed to be stored may play a part in determining serial cut-off dates. At Rice University, for example, all print runs of periodicals will be stored according to this schedule: Science and engineering journals, pre-1980; Social and behavioral science periodicals pre-1970; Humanities (including history) pre-1960. These dates were used in order to reduce enough volumes in the stacks for future renovation to occur. Although the Indiana University Bloomington Libraries mandated each branch reduce its collections by 20%, they did not specify format.[34]

In addition, each library is unique and has specific goals for their storage facilities as well as their on-campus libraries. The academic institutions that have remote storage vary in many aspects–size of student population, whether public or private, in a consortial or single institution storage setting, programs of study offered, a unified campus library or multiple libraries, and physical location, i.e., big city or small town. Storage impacts patrons' work quality, productivity and convenience, splits collections, and may possibly lead to a decline in usage.[35] However, a 3-tiered hierarchy tends to emerge of the types of materials relegated to storage. First the library seeks to remove those materials with the least impact, e.g., duplicate copies, out-dated texts, etc. Next, or concurrently, journal runs are targeted due to the amount of space that can be recaptured relatively quickly and easily. The last stage, item-by-item selection, is often the most difficult and contentious issue.

For item-by-item selection, libraries may benefit from the use of standard catalogs and listings in making their evaluations. ALA's

Books for College Libraries,[36] Choice's *Opening Day Collection*,[37] specialized bibliographies, print catalogs of important or specialized libraries, lists of authorized works from professional associations, the most cited journals in *Journal Citation Reports*,[38] books and journals covered by indexing and abstracting services, course syllabi, and current acquisitions lists of specialized libraries are among the types of evaluation tools that can be used and should be included in the collection development policy.

Cornell University's website has an excellent example of the variations in the percentages of monographs and serials sent to storage by each branch (subject) library on its page entitled *Annex Expansion Project: Summary of Selection Methods and Quantity of Material by Library*. The Fine Arts Library sent 37,150 volumes to storage of which 100% were monographs while the Engineering Library sent 93,000 volumes of which 27% were serials, 45% monographs, and 28% were multi-volume monographs and the Management Library sent 45,900 volumes of which 65% were serials. Additionally, the branch libraries varied in selection methods, some using an item-by-item evaluation in the stacks while others selected from computer generated lists of materials published since 1992 that had not circulated using the online system.[39]

SPECIFIC CRITERIA FOR SELECTION

Circulation Statistics

There are several factors to consider when using this criterion, primarily the number of years for which data is available and the accuracy of the statistics. Data on materials circulated before the availability of online systems will not be captured and institutions may not have collected in-house statistics that can greatly change the perception of use. This is true especially of serials whose circulation is generally restricted.

Duplicates

Removing duplicate copies of a title is an easy, sensible, and safe beginning point.[40] When selecting duplicates for storage not only the number of duplicate copies but how often each copy has circulated may be important.[41] Care must be taken to review circulation statistics and course offerings to assess user demand for multiple copies. If the duplication occurs among two or more library branches, which one will send its copy to storage if at all? Should the existence of informal departmental libraries be included in the decision-making?

Materials Duplicated in Other Formats or Library Branches

Newspapers and popular journals, such as the New York Times may exist in a library in bound, microform, and digital format. Current issues may be received in paper and discarded when the microfilm arrives while backfiles are available through ProQuest and current issues from several online vendors. Thus, the decision as to what to store and in what format can take on multiple dimensions. For multi-library campuses where two or more branches subscribe to the same title, an agreement may have to be made as to which library will retain the physical item.

Out-of-Date Works

Travel guidebooks, scientific and technical works are good candidates for storage. Some of these materials may merit de-accessioning, depending on the curriculum. An institution with a recreation, tourism, or hospitality emphasis may want to retain travel books for historical research. Universities and colleges with an emphasis on the historical aspects of science may also want to retain out-of-date works to track the development of the discipline.

Superseded or Revised Texts

Again, depending on the curricular and research needs, superseded or revised texts may have no interest to your patrons, or they may be an important source for research. Faculty interested in the history of their field use old texts to track its development. Older legal materials, however, may not be of interest on campus and could give patrons false or misleading information if they are relied on.

Materials of a Non-Academic Nature

Most libraries have been gifted or purchased works of a non-academic nature, for example, juvenile literature, popular works, or inspirational literature. Similarly, works published by non-mainstream publishers or otherwise of questionable research value are candidates for weeding or storage.

Ceased, Cancelled, or Non-Indexed Serials

The rationale for storing serials that have ceased or cancelled is that, presumably, they are not as valuable as on-going publications. They should be carefully reviewed for relevance to academic programs before being relegated to storage. Serials for which no indexing exists are also good candidates since the articles would not be found through conventional means.

Obsolete Formats

Technology's Achilles heal is the rapid change of formats. Reel-to-reel tapes, filmstrips, microcard, floppy discs, 8-tracks, 3/4" tape, and LPs have all seen their "15 minutes of fame." Often equipment that can play these formats does not exist in the library or no longer works. They are obvious candidates for storage, from both the preservation and technological standpoints.

Reference Value

Is the work used as a reference tool? If used primarily for quick look-ups, it may be best to retain in the active collection, to avoid long retrieval delays to look up or verify information. Such works as the *Statistical Abstract of the United States* are superseded each year, yet a strong argument could be made for the merit of keeping past volumes in the active collection. It has been suggested that libraries should retain its runs of titles that are used primarily for quick look-ups.[42] Is it still necessary to keep print copies of national bibliographies, print catalogs of collections, and the *Mansell's* or *NUC's* with the advent of electronic access to holdings? Other books of a bibliographic nature pose similar difficulties. Are old subject bibliographies superseded by the ease of searching electronic databases? The answer to these questions will vary by institutional need. Using this argument, some libraries may decide to that large, seldom used works such as statistical compilations should not be relegated to storage.[43]

Variant Editions

Variant editions of the same work pose an interesting dilemma. In some cases the text is the same among editions though the introductory or explanatory material is by different scholars. Knowing the curriculum and working with the faculty will help decide the necessity of keeping any or all of the variant editions of *The Adventures of Huckleberry Finn*. Variant translations, particularly of the Bible and the classics, may need to be retained for comparative value. Similarly, variant texts of major works such as Shakespeare or facsimile editions of manuscripts, may need to be retained for the use of scholars.

Foreign Language Materials

Materials in foreign languages not supported by the University are another candidate for storage. This may include both literary and non-literary works. Adequate coverage of a topic in English or foreign language texts on subjects not related to that language, country, or culture may justify removal of non-literary works in foreign languages.[44] However, texts of laws, diplomatic documents, or other works that may be significant for research should be retained in the native language. What about translations of works from English? Foreign language translations of original English language texts may be valuable for research on a particular author or for comparison of translations.

Rarity

There are thousands of works on library shelves that should be in a rare book or special collection. The pre-1900 Serial Set is one example. Because it is voluminous, many special collection departments lack the space to house it. Cages offer protection against theft or vandalism but lack the environmental controls these materials may require. Preservation is a strong argument in favor of remote storage that the library needs to promote.

Physical Condition

This criterion is the best argument in favor of storage as it makes preservation the primary consideration. There will be items for which the controlled environment of the storage facility comes too late. How much time, effort, and money a library puts into conservation will separate between items fit for storage and those that should either be reformatted or discarded.

Age of the Material

Some universities have used the age, i.e., copyright or imprint date of a book as a cut-off point. The date any individual library uses depends on the length of time the library has been collecting, the amount of material to be used, and the discipline involved. The University of Michigan, in its first wave of selection, choose to review "Monographs published through 1800 . . . " and "Books published between 1870-1949 . . ." primarily for preservation purposes,[45] Not all academic libraries will have collections or significant numbers of materials of so early a vintage. Often a cut-off date is selected in combination with circulation statistics to determine if it is a candidate for storage. The various branches of the Cornell University libraries used different cut-off dates for monographs and serials depending on the discipline(s) each library supported.[46]

Material Peripheral to Current Curricular and Research Interests

Academic disciplines may have shifted focus or libraries may have received extra funding to support areas of research that are no longer of research interest. Libraries may have excellent collections in areas not related to the curriculum as a result of gifts or past interests. Moving this material to storage helps to keep the active collection focused. Some studies suggest that a more focused collection is easier to use and maintain.[47] Since library funds were used to purchase this material, relegating it to storage may be an ideal solution.

Artifactual Value

There are several different ways of defining a work's "artifactual" value. It could be valuable as an example of a binding, typeface, or printer's design. Or, it could be valuable for the plates or illustrations it contains. Many an expensive art book has been razored to death for its illustrations. Maps and recordings are also vulnerable to intentional and unintentional damage. While not qualifying for special collections designation (or no space for it), these items may well qualify for storage.

CONCLUSION

The development of off-site storage in the academic environment has been controversial. President Charles Eliot of Harvard debated the issues with Harvard Librarian Lane during Harvard's first move into remote storage in 1900. The issues surrounding remote storage were and still are, (a) the economics of storage versus unimpeded access, (b) lack of agreement on how to predict what books will be used, and (c) the interplay between faculty and librarians regarding choice of materials.[48]

While unpopular, remote storage is practical from economic, preservation, and security viewpoints. Therefore a collection development policy needs to be established to insure fairness in the way the materials are selected for storage. Fairness does not mean that all disciplines will relegate to storage the same number of items or percentages. Some disciplines may relegate more, some disciplines less. Fairness does mean eliciting and *using* faculty input. It does mean keeping discipline specific needs in mind. It does mean having a rationale for decision-making, retaining institutional memory, and selecting according to collection goals to ensure consistency over time.

There are many aspects to determining what general and specific criteria to use for a particular library. While in many cases general and specific criteria overlap, general criteria are those that will be applied by the library across disciplines or types of material. Specific criteria are those that define the exceptions necessary to accommodate individual disciplines, library collections, or campus needs. In the end, it comes down to the library's individual situation. However, faculty involvement and a written collection development policy will go a long way toward making the best choices as to which materials should go to storage and which should not.

REFERENCES

1. Nicholson Baker, *Double Fold: Libraries and the Assault on Paper.* (NY: Random House, 2001).

2. *Ibid.*, p.136.

3. David Block, "Remote Storage in Research Libraries: A Microhistory," *Library Resources and Technical Services*, 44, no. 4 (Oct. 2000) p. 184.

4. Dan Hazen, "Selecting for Storage: Local Problems, Local Responses, and an Emerging Common Challenge," *Library Resources and Technical Services*, 44, no. 4 (Oct. 2000) p. 176.

5. Block, "Remote Storage," p. 187.

6. *Ibid.*, p. 186.

7. Kenneth E. Carpenter and Jeffrey L. Horrell. "A Harvard Experience." in Danuta A. Nitecki and Curtis L. Kendrick, eds. *Library Off-Site Shelving: Guide for High-Density Facilities.* (Littleton, CO: Libraries Unlimited, 2001).

8. Jean Dickinson, "If the Book Doesn't Fit . . . Managing a Library Storage Facility: A Report of the LAMA Buildings and Equipment Section Preconference," *Library Collections, Acquisitions, and Technical Services* 24, no. 2 (Summer 2000) p. 277.

9. Lee Ash, *Yale's Selective Book Retirement Program.* (Hamden, CT: Archon Books, 1963).

10. Herman H. Fussler and Julian L. Simon, *Patterns in the Use of Books in Large Research Libraries*. (Chicago: University of Chicago Press, 1969).

11. Allen Kent et al., *Use of Library Materials: the University of Pittsburgh Study*. (New York: Marcel Dekker, 1979).

12. Stanley J. Slote. *Weeding Library Collections: Library Weeding Methods*. 4th ed. (Englewood, CO: Libraries Unlimited, 1997) pp. 61-62.

13. *Ibid*, p. 63.

14. *Ibid*, pp. 73-75.

15. Margaret K. Powell, "The Yale University Libraries Experience." in Danuta A. Nitecki and Curtis L. Kendrick, ed. *Library Off-Site Shelving: Guide for High-Density Facilities*. (Littleton, CO: Libraries Unlimited, 2001) p. 133.

16. Robert S. Seeds, "Impact of Remote Library Storage on Information Consumers: 'Sophie's Choice'?" *Collection Building* 19 no. 3 (2000) p. 107.

17. J. B. Hill, Cherie Madarash-Hill, and Nancy Hayes, "Remote Storage of Serials: Its Impact on Use," *The Serials Librarian*, 39, no. 1 (2000) p. 38.

18. Hazen, "Selecting for Storage," p. 180.

19. Powell, "Yale University Libraries Experience," pp. 135-136.

20. Hazen, "Selecting for Storage," p. 180.

21. *Ibid*, p. 187.

22. Powell, "Yale University Libraries Experience," p. 132.

23. Dickinson, "If the Book Doesn't Fit," p. 280.

24. Hazen, "Remote Storage in Research Libraries," p. 179.

25. Sheila S. Intner, "Why Written Collection Development Policies Are Important," *Technicalities* 16, no. 7 (1996) p. 10.

26. Jack G. Montgomery, "Of Tossing Books, There Is No End." *Against the Grain*, 68.

27. Lenore Clark, ed., *Guide to Review of Library Collections: Preservation, Storage, and Withdraw*. (Chicago: American Library Association, 1991).

28. Barbara Lockett, ed., *Guide to the Evaluation of Library Collections* (Chicago: American Library Association, 1989).

29. Slote, *Weeding Library Collections*.

30. Seeds, "Impact of Remote Library Storage on Information Consumers," p. 106.

31. Kenneth E. Carpenter and Jeffrey L. Horrell, "A Harvard Experience," in Danuta A. Nitecki and Curtis L. Kendrick, ed. *Library Off-Site Shelving: Guide for High-Density Facilities*. (Littleton, CO: Libraries Unlimited, 2001) p. 128.

32. Carpenter and Horrell, "A Harvard Experience." p. 128.

33. Powell, "Yale University Libraries Experience," p. 139.

34. Indian University Web Site: www.indiana.edu/%7Elibweb/alf/guidelines.html.

35. Scott Seaman and Donna DeGeorge, "Selecting and Moving Books to a Remote Depository: A Case Study." *Collection Management* 16, no. 1 (1992) pp. 137-142.

36. *Books for College Libraries: A Core Collection of 50,000 Titles*, 3rd ed. (Chicago: American Library Association, 1988).

37. Richard K. Gardner and Louise F. Lockwood, eds. *Opening Day Collection*, 3rd ed. (Middletown, CT: Choice, 1974).

38. *Journal Citation Reports on CD-ROM* (Philadelphia: Institute for Scientific Information, 1995-).

39. Cornell University Web Site. www.library.cornell.edu/newannex/materials.htm.

40. Seeds, "Impact of Remote Library Storage" p. 105.

41. Seaman & DeGeorge, p. 139.

42. Carpenter and Horrell, "A Harvard Experience," p. 128.

43. *Ibid*, p. 127.
44. *Ibid*, p. 126.
45. Wendy P. Longee, "Remote Storage Comes of Age: Storage Collection Management at the University of Michigan," *Collection Management* 16, no. 2 (1992) p. 96.
46. Cornell University Web Site: www.library.cornell/edu/newannex/materials.htm.
47. Slote, *Weeding Library Collections*, p. 4-5.
48. Block, "Remote Storage," p. 184.

Collection Development: Curriculum Materials Center

Justina O. Osa

SUMMARY. This article attempts to touch on very practical aspects of developing and maintaining instructional materials for the curriculum materials center. The main focus of the article is a description of the many activities and issues the instructional materials librarian has to attend to as he/she builds and manages collections that support teacher education programs. The author presents a brief discussion of basic activities the librarian undertakes before selecting instructional materials, while selecting the materials, and after the materials are acquired. The article also includes a short description of the different types of instructional materials that are often selected for the curriculum materials center. *[Article copies available for a fee from The Haworth Document Delivery Service: 1-800-HAWORTH. E-mail address: <docdelivery@haworthpress.com> Website: <http://www.HaworthPress.com> © 2003 by The Haworth Press, Inc. All rights reserved.]*

KEYWORDS. Collection development, library materials development, instructional material selection, curriculum materials center, instructional materials, library material selection, instructional materials centers, learning resources centers, curriculum materials, library acquisition

Justina O. Osa is Education Librarian, The Pennsylvania State University Libraries, Education & Behavioral Sciences Library, E-502C Paterno Library, University Park, PA 16802 (E-mail: joo2@psu.edu).

[Haworth co-indexing entry note]: "Collection Development: Curriculum Materials Center." Osa, Justina O. Co-published simultaneously in *The Acquisitions Librarian* (The Haworth Information Press, an imprint of The Haworth Press, Inc.) No. 30, 2003, pp. 131-153; and: *Collection Development Policies: New Directions for Changing Collections* (ed: Daniel C. Mack) The Haworth Information Press, an imprint of The Haworth Press, Inc., 2003, pp. 131-153. Single or multiple copies of this article are available for a fee from The Haworth Document Delivery Service [1-800-HAWORTH, 9:00 a.m. - 5:00 p.m. (EST). E-mail address: docdelivery@haworthpress.com].

http://www.haworthpress.com/store/product.asp?sku=J101
© 2003 by The Haworth Press, Inc. All rights reserved.
10.1300/J101v15n30_11

This article attempts to provide a practical perspective on developing collections for the teacher education programs. This collection goes by different names such as Curriculum Development Center, Instructional Materials Collection, Instructional Materials and Textbooks Collection, Curriculum Materials Center, and Learning Resources Center. In spite of the different terms they all mean basically the same thing because they all focus on collections that support teacher education programs and instructional materials that assist faculty and prospective teachers to effectively teach topics in the curriculum. "Curriculum materials are physical entities, representational in nature, used to facilitate the learning process. The term, physical entities, means that curriculum materials are observable objects, not ideas and concepts . . . The representational nature of curriculum materials means that they signify something other than themselves . . . [and] distinguishes them from curriculum supplies."[1]

Developing and managing materials for the Instructional Materials Center have assumed more importance in recent years. The increased interest in the quality of the collection and its uses could be attributed largely to the increased demand for accountability in teacher preparation and the constant demand for student achievement especially at the K-12 schools. Prospective teachers are being progressively required to create the best possible learning environment for their students and to be skilled in creating new ways to inspire every student to learn and to reach his/her full potential. One of the questions NCATE suggests in an article "What to Look for in a Teacher Preparation Program" is "Does the institution have the resources necessary to support each of the programs it offers?"[2] Additionally, "NCATE standards also expect teacher educators to model effective teaching. The traditional lecture alone is inadequate. Teacher educators must use strategies that they expect their candidates to use. Why? Teachers teach as they are taught. Teacher educators should model expert teaching."[3] Teachers are central to education, and are expected to be skilled in actually letting theory inform their actual in-class instructional activities. Knowing the content and presenting it in such a way that only some "smart" students learn is no longer enough. The focus is on assisting all students to learn by packaging the same concept in varied ways that make it possible for the teacher to reach all students irrespective of their diverse characteristics. This could be a colossal task for the classroom teacher. Gone are the days when teachers were taught to teach in a hypothetical or theoretical environment. Teacher education majors must now undergo training that makes teacher preparation a real world experience.

National and international attention have been focused and is still being focused on training teachers who are competent enough to be placed in the classrooms. Numerous and different strategies have been adopted to get prospective teachers prepared to teach effectively in schools. These include required core courses, required method courses, early field experiences, practicum or practica, and portfolio development.

Educators and parents would like to see every child achieve academically in school. This will not happen until there is a fit across materials, learners, and teachers. When adequate instructional materials in all formats are available for teachers and students to use, the possibility of the teacher succeeding in helping all students learn is higher. But the mere presence of adequate instructional materials is not enough. Teacher education majors need to be exposed to these materials, see their instructors/professors model integrating them into in-class instructional activities, and have assignments that demand that prospective teachers identify and use these materials in completing assignments and in lesson plan development and lesson delivery. They should acquire the knowledge and skills to provide, plan, and deliver lessons that offer varied ways for students to engage in the cognitive, affective, and psychomotor domains of the contents of the lessons. Teacher education majors have to be trained to be reflective practitioners who continually identify, use, and evaluate the effects of their instructional material choices on student learning. They must use instructional strategies to create learning environments that promote active learning for all students.

The education librarian who has the responsibility to choose high quality materials relevant to the objectives and processes of the teacher education programs has a significantly important task. There are some vital factors that would assist him/her as he/she builds and maintains the teacher education collections. These include a knowledge and awareness of:

- Educational theory, practice, and philosophy
- Current issues and reforms in education
- The teacher education programs in his/her institution
- The certification and degree requirements for teacher education majors
- Instructional materials available for purchase or/and access
- Skills necessary to satisfactorily evaluate the material to determine suitability for selection and deselection.

BEFORE SELECTING INSTRUCTIONAL MATERIALS

There are some basic activities the librarian should undertake before selecting instructional materials. "Would you tell me, please, said Alice, which way I ought to walk from here? That depends a good deal on where you want to get to, said the cat" (Carroll, 1941). The librarian must have a clear understanding of the type of collection he/she must build. The importance of a collection development manual that contains collection development statements, goals, policies, and procedures cannot be overemphasized. They are the factors that become the roadmap, the compass, and the force that guides and drives the decisions and activities of the librarian as he/she develops the instructional materials and enables the librarian to know what the thrust of the collection is or is not going to be. The main focus of all collection development activities should be acquiring and making readily available and accessible, quality materials to prepare prospective teachers to meet both their degree and certification requirements. The collection development policy should include information to address general collection selection criteria such as the scope of the collection, collection levels, treatment of subject, language, types and formats of materials, diversity, exclusions, chronology, and cost. The collection development could also address issues such as approval plan, patrons to be served, non-print materials, gifts, resource sharing, circulation and access issues, mutilated, stolen and lost items, replacement, maintenance, and weeding. It is vital that the librarian realizes that collection development policy is a document that should frequently be reviewed and revised because it is a document that is always in transition.

Needs Assessment

Needs assessment is the first step in the process of building and maintaining strong instructional materials collections to support the teacher education programs and to meet the needs of all the potential users of the collections. Needs assessment serves as a systematic diagnostic tool to carefully and to cautiously identify what the clienteles need, what the thrust of the collection should be, and what the librarian should be doing to effectively and efficiently meet patrons' needs. The librarian needs to know if the current collections are at the ideal or desired level, or if there are discrepancies between the current collections and the ideal collections, and know if and how he/she needs to strategically plan to remedy the discrepancies in the collections. Some of the activities involved in needs assessment include:

- Environmental scan
- Analysis of available records and statistics on instructional materials
- Analysis of the information gathered from the suggestion box
- Survey
- Interviews of different focus groups that make up the potential clienteles
- Accessing and using relevant information either separately stated or integrated into the standards of the appropriate professional associations and accreditation bodies that state the acceptable levels of library collections and services
- Familiarity with current trends, issues, and practices in the field of teacher education and instruction material collections and
- Evaluation of the instructional materials collections.

The librarian could enhance the quality and effectiveness of the materials selected if prior to selecting he/she:

1. Knows the programs the collection is to support
2. Knows who will use the collection
3. Knows how the collection will be used
4. Assesses the collection and identifies its adequacy
5. Recognizes gaps and areas of needs in the current collection based on deficiency
6. Knows the amount in the budget that is devoted to instructional materials
7. Has knowledge of locating and verifying tools such as catalogs, bibliographies, web sites, databases, and publication announcements
8. Knows and uses reviewing sources
9. Is aware of publication announcement and selection tools provided by professional associations and committees
10. Recognizes when to request for copies for preview
11. Knows when to solicit expert opinion from faculty and senior colleagues on the quality and appropriateness of the item being considered for acquisition

SELECTING INSTRUCTIONAL MATERIALS

Selection is at the heart of the collection development process. "Collection development has always been about making choices."[4] Making the choice of which materials to select and which ones not to select has been a large and arduous task. Good and informed choices guarantee high quality instructional materials for teacher education programs. The prime criterion for selecting an instructional material is embedded in librarians' responses to three critical questions:

1. Will this instructional material help students learn?
2. Will it reinforce the concepts learned?
3. Will it expand learning for students?

The librarian should ensure that he/she follows the guidelines stated in the collection development manual. In addition to these guidelines it would be useful for the librarian to evaluate the contents of the materials to be selected. Quality is a crucial factor in instructional materials collections. The content and quality of the instructional materials influence what students learn and how well they learn the instructional concepts. The materials should be evaluated and assessed for quality and appropriateness of the:

1. Information
2. Subject discipline
3. Content to the intended clientele
4. Treatment of subject
5. Coverage both in scope and depth
6. Special features

There are some other additional criteria that should always guide the selection of instructional materials. Materials to be integrated into the instructional materials collection should:

- Make the concept or skill to be learned meaningful
- Stimulate and spark students' interest
- Motivate and inspire students to learn
- Teach and/or reinforce concepts or skills
- Enhance progress and celebrate accomplishment

The presentation and the physical characteristics of the instructional materials to be selected should be colorful, attractive, and able to grab students' interest and to ignite their curiosity.

Types of Instructional Materials Often Selected

Text Books

These days text books are being used more judiciously. They do not determine the scope and sequence of study as they used to do. Text books are increasingly being used as resource tools in conjunction with their resources. Most instructional material centers acquire text books in all subject areas, and appropriate for all levels from P-12 grades. They also feature state approved or/and state adopted text books. Those adopted by the local school districts are often acquired comprehensively while those for other districts and states are selectively acquired. The rationale for their inclusion is that both instructors/professors and prospective teachers should know the state adopted text books, become familiar with them as the teacher education faculty integrate them into their syllabi, and as teacher education majors consult them for assignment completion and for preparing for their early field experiences and practica. It is believed that when prospective teachers are familiar with the state approved text books they will be more successful in using these materials when they go out to the Professional Development Schools (PDS) for clinical teaching. There are also subject-matter units that cover specific subjects and are used in class as texts.

Curricular Guides

These are vital components of the instructional materials centers. Curriculum guides focus on the organized and intended topics and experiences designed for students and are often arranged in developmental appropriate sequence. They often include instructional goals, objectives, outcomes, major concepts of each phase, instructional strategies, resource listings, suggestions for presenting the instructional theme, and assessment criteria and conditions. Just like approved and adopted text books, the curricular guides for the local schools are acquired comprehensively while those for other school districts are acquired selectively.

Standards

"Standards are exemplary performances that serve as a benchmark."[5] The content standards for all subject areas are criteria to judge quality and to promote excellence. National standards encourage policies that will bring coordination, consistency, and coherence. They describe outcomes which are what students should understand and be able to do at the end of a unit, or grade level completion. Standards do not usually state the manner in which students will achieve those outcomes. There are national, state, regional, and local school district standards. They are crucial resources. Copies of standards should be acquired for the instructional materials center.

Puzzles

Puzzles are an essential part of a child's development. They are fun and they foster creativity and problem solving skills in young learners. Puzzles enable young learners to learn and to master trial and error techniques and to learn persistence as they create a sense of order out of disorder, and see how parts and pieces of an object join together to form a whole.

Standardized Tests

Librarians are of different and varied opinions when it comes to the inclusion of standardized tests in the instructional materials collection. The philosophy of the library or/and the parent institution would determine if standardized tests would be included in the collection.

Teacher Certification Test

The main goal of tests in teacher preparation is to guarantee quality and equity. It has been said that these tests serve as gate keepers to keep students who would like to major in teacher education out of the teacher education programs. Often admission into the teacher education profession unit in teacher colleges or schools of education is based on students scoring at the acceptable level on the teachers tests. The librarian would be doing a good service to the education program by making the best teachers' test preparation materials available in the instructional materials collections. Educational Testing Service (ETS) is recognized as the world's most experienced educational testing and measurement organization. Examples of their products include the Praxis Series: Professional Assessments for Beginning Teachers which is a set of tests that most teacher education programs use to admit students into the programs. Most state education departments use these tests in making teacher licensing decisions. Praxis I: Academic Skills Assessments is used to admit students into a teacher education program. Praxis II: Subject Assessments is used for licensure for entering the teaching profession. Praxis III: Classroom Performance Assessments is used for assessing first year teachers. REA (Research & Education Association) is another recognized body that markets reputable study aids and test preparation materials for teacher education majors. An example of their products is *The Best Teachers' Test Preparation for PRAXIS PLT Test, Grades 7-12: Principles of Learning and Teaching Test.* It is designed to help student success and make good scores. On the cover of the item it states that it covers all essential information on the examination, every examination question is answered with detailed explanations, proven test-taking tips to help students make top score.

Recordings

The recordings often integrated into the instructional materials collection are audio cassettes, video cassettes, films, and compact discs. They constitute a very popular group of materials among teacher education faculty and students. They are used on a regular basis to: set induction; introduce key ideas; motivate students; provide information; encourage class discussions, small or large group discussions; and to promote inductive and divergent thinking.

Manipulatives and Kits

The use of manipulatives and kits promotes the construction of knowledge by students. They are often accompanied with activity guides, step-by-step instructions on how to use the kits, and suggestions to facilitate activities and exercises completion.

Multimedia

These are items with information in more than one type of format. They may come in the form of a combination of print and non-print items such as a book with audio or video cassettes, compact discs, manipulatives, or transparencies.

Juvenile Materials

Some curriculum material centers also support the Language and Literacy Education (LL Ed) programs. Such centers usually collect children's books, juvenile fiction and non-fiction, picture books, large books, lap books, and other special titles such as the Newbery and Caldecott award winning books, notable and honor titles.

Activities and Idea Books

These are materials that offer and suggest the ideas and activities that enhance the effectiveness of instruction. They encourage hands-on learning and make learning fun, pleasant, and interesting. The activities are often presented in such a way that is flexible enough for the teacher to tailor to meet the needs of the particular classroom and group of students the teacher is working with. Activities books usually include reproducibles which teachers can photocopy for student use. There are frequently full instructions or guides for use for both teacher and students. An example of an activities book is *The Discovery of the Americas: Activities Book* which was written by Betsy and Giulio Maestro to accompany their work–*The Discovery of the Americas*. Another example is *The United States, Its History and Neighbors* which is comprised of eight volumes–student text, teacher's edition, teacher's edition activity book, activity book, extension activities tests, picture posters, overhead transparencies with copying masters, and the map book.

Transparencies

These are instructional illustrations designed for projection. They are often accompanied with other instructional materials such as study guides, text, and narration stored in audio cassettes.

Flash Cards

These are usually used to teach concepts to students in lower grades. In foreign languages and English as a Second Language (ESL) programs flash cards could be of awesome value. They feature objects students are familiar with and they facilitate the learning of new vocabulary, new pronunciation, and can be used to encourage students to build sentences about the picture on the card or cards, and to work in small groups. They can also be used as drill exercises. An example is *Photo Flash Cards: Clothing Nouns*. The word for the object is provided on the reverse side of the flash card in English, French, Spanish, and German. Instructions on how to use the flash cards are included.

Simulations and Games

Simulations and games are inspiring learning tools. "Simulation and games can be defined roughly as a series of activities in a sequence, in which players participate, which has stated rules, usually involving competition and leading towards an objective."[6] Simulations and games enable students to function in a situation that is similar to the real situation. Students have the opportunity to have direct interaction with the concept to be learned, become active learners, and to acquire the concept by doing. Most of the present day students belong to the Nintendo generation. They find it pleasurable to learn by connections pieces of information that lead to learning as they complete challenging activities. Skill-building games such as *Let's Go Shopping!*, let students develop money mathematics skills as they go shopping and practice concepts such as addition, subtraction, multiplication, and division.

Dioramas

A diorama is a "three-dimensional representation of a scene created by placing objects, figures, etc., in front of a two-dimensional painted background."[7] Artifacts and artifact reproductions are used to recreate or display concepts. An example of a diorama is *Grinding Corn: Hopi.* It is a diorama put together by W.P.A. Museum Extension Projects. Artifact reproductions are used to create a scene that depicts Hopi Indians grinding corn. This diorama enable the students to vividly and to visually see lifestyle change among the Hopi Indians.

Posters and Charts

Posters and charts are colorful, attractive learning media that make learning fun. An example is *How Plants Make Food.* The poster gives a short introduction on how plants make food. The six steps of the process of photosynthesis are described in simple language. There are four reproducibles on the reverse side of the poster. They are: Nature's Food Factory; Plant Facts; Autumn Color Change; and Plants We Eat. The Brainwork is also provided to stimulate students' critical thinking.

Models

Models are realistic and authentic representations. They are used to enhance student learning of fundamental concepts. Human Heart is an example of models that are ideal for the science classroom. It is made up of four parts and it shows the various structures of the human heart. The top section can be disconnected to display the interior parts of the human heart. The identified structures are labeled corresponding to terms listed in the accompanying guide. There are also two model arteries or veins that can be attached to the heart to replicate the real heart.

Monographs

The ETS (Educational Testing Services) study "How Teaching Matters" found not surprisingly that subject matter knowledge is important. Specifically, the study finds that student achievement increases by 40 percent of a grade level in both math and science when teachers have a major or minor in the subject taught.[8] Consequently the librarian has to select some relevant monographs that focus on topics, subjects, issues, and trends that are of interest to teacher education programs. The depth of subject treatment should be of significant importance when selecting monographs.

Electronic Resources

Instructional materials centers now collect electronic resources because of the invasion of new technologies in the information arena. Examples of electronic resources include computer software, course specific web pages, topic specific web pages, online tutorials, and guides.

Songs for Teaching

Increasingly, music is being creatively used to teach instructional content in the classrooms. Songs could be a faster medium to teach some concepts. The librarian should include song books and collections of songs that teach. Some examples of such songs include:

Captain Vegetable

Out of his secret garden somewhere in New Jersey comes your newest favorite super hero!
It is I, Captain Vegetable With my carrot, and my celery
Eating crunchy vegetables is good for me, And they're good for you, so eat them too
For teeth so strong, your whole life long Eat celery and carrots by the bunch
Three cheers for me, Captain Vegetable Crunch, crunch, crunch!

Gee, Captain Vegetable this is the best thing to come around since meatballs!
Three cheers for Captain Vegetable! Three cheers for me Captain Vegetable
Crunch crunch crunch!

Used with permission.

Vegetables (Sung to "Mary Had a Little Lamb")

We are pumpkins, big and round Big and round, big and round
We are pumpkins, big and round Seated on the ground.
We are string beans, green and fine. . . . Growing on a vine.
We are onions, round and white. . . . we make soup taste right.
We are carrots, orange and long . . . Help us sing our song.
We are cabbage, green or red. . . . See our funny head.
We are corn stalks, tall and straight. . . . Don't we just taste great.

Used with permission.

Songs that teach are very useful in language classes. For example Alouette is a fun song that facilitates the teaching of the parts of the body in French to non-French speaking students. The teacher and students point to each part of the body as they sing.[9]

Alouette

Alouette, gentille Alouette Alouette, je te plumerai.
Je te plumerai la tête Je te plumerai la tête
Et la tête, (girls) Et la tête, (boys)
Alouette, (girls) Alouette, (boys) O-o-o . . .
Alouette, gentille Alouette,
Alouette, je te plumerai.
Je te plumerai le bec, Je te plumerai le bec, Et la tête, (girls) Et la tête, (boys) Et le bec, (girls)
Et le bec, (boys) Alouette, (girls) Alouette, (boys)
O-o-o . . .

Continue with . . .

le cou, le dos, les ailes, la queue, les jambs, les pieds [Just a few notes of interest–"alouette" translates as lark or skylark. So, the lyrics translate as: Skylark, sweet skylark, I will pluck you; I will pluck your head, beak, neck, back, wings, knees, feet.][10]

Reference Materials

These are materials that are not intended for cover to cover reading. They are materials that are expected to be referred to for specific information. The scope could be broad or narrow, regional, national, or international. Reference materials for the instructional materials center includes handbooks, encyclopedias–general, subject or topic-specific encyclopedias, dictionaries–general, topic or discipline-specific dictionaries, yearbooks, guides, historical sources, biographical sources, statistical sources, works on tests and measurements, and directories, thesauruses, catalogs, indexes, abstracts, reviews, and government documents on education-related issues, trends and topics. The librarian may also in addition to these print sources develop bookmarks of useful electronic reference sites that cover topics of interest for teacher educators, teachers, and parents.

Periodicals

There are some journals that should be found in the instructional materials collection. *The Journal of Teacher Education*–features articles on teacher education research and practice, and articles on varied views on currently relevant issues. *The Journal of Teacher Education*–covers social and professional issues affecting teachers at all levels. *Journal of Curriculum Studies*–publishes papers which address the many questions surrounding issues of theory, policymaking, and practice in all areas of curriculum and teaching for elementary and secondary schools, and for teacher education institutions. *Copycat*–features ideas and activities for K-3 teachers. *Creative Classroom*–presents hands-on teaching techniques for the Pre K-6 teachers. *The Elementary School Journal* offers articles on curriculum, behaviors, and interactions of teachers and students at the elementary level. *Instructor*–features articles on a wide range of topics of interest to elementary school teachers. *The Mailbox*–offers numerous ideas to help teachers make learning fun for students in Pre K-6. *Teaching Pre K-8*–focuses on articles that present classroom-tested methods and ideas appropriate for teachers in Pre K-8. *Social Studies and the Young Learner*–publishes articles on creative teaching in grades K-6. *The Journal of Educational Research*–features scholarly works of authors who experiment with new procedures, evaluate traditional practices, replicate previous research for validation, and perform other work central to understanding and improving the education of today's students and educators. *Journal for Research in Mathe-*

matics Education–focuses on research reports and reviews on the teaching and learning of mathematics at all levels. *The Quarterly Journal of Music Teaching and Learning*–serves as a clearinghouse for ideas among professors of music education. *International Journal of Science Education*–provides information, ideas and opinions that serve as a means for placing research findings in the context of the classroom. *Journal of Elementary Science Education*–focuses on research on learning and teaching science in elementary school. *Journal of Science Teacher Education*–serves as a forum for disseminating research and theoretical position statements concerning the preparation and in-service education of science teachers. *Curriculum Inquiry*–carries articles on studies of curriculum development and evaluation, school reform, educational theory and practice, classrooms, and teaching. *AIMS* (Activities Integrating Mathematics and Science) provides ideas to enrich the education of students in K-9. Hands-on activities integrate mathematics, science, and other disciplines.

Databases

There are some crucial and significant databases which the librarian should subscribe to. Their main focus is on education. The Educational Resources Information Center (ERIC) database is the world's largest source of education information to teachers, librarians, counselors, administrators, parents, and anyone interested in education throughout the United States and the world.[11] This database contains more than one million abstracts of education-related documents and journal articles. Kraus Curriculum Development Library Online (KCDLOnline) is a searchable database that provides users with curriculum information on a variety of subjects covered in Pre K-12 and Adult Basic Education. This searchable database of curricula, frameworks, and standards brings together educational objectives, content, instructional strategies, and evaluative techniques for all subjects covered in Pre K-12 and Adult Basic Education. It is indexed for easy access. KCDLOnline used to be reproduced on microfiche, but now it is available online. Children's Literature Comprehensive Database offers information about children's books, videos, and audio books ranging from baby board books to novels and nonfiction for young adults. The database contains 700,000 MARC format records and includes 110,000 full text book reviews from well-respected sources such as *KIRKUS Reviews, Science Books & Films*, and *Voice of Youth Advocates (VOYA)*.

Gifts

There are very limited opportunities to build the instructional materials collection with gift items. This could be attributed to the peculiar nature of the collections. The collection development manual should cover policies and procedures for accepting, rejecting, and for handling gifts. Only gift items that complement and enhance the collections should be accepted. Gift items that are made up of multiple parts or pieces should be complete. Quality should not be ignored just because items are gifts.

Provide Access

The responsibilities of the librarian do not stop with selecting and acquiring instructional materials. He/she must organize, preserve, and provide access to the selected materials. Some of the decisions the librarian must deal with while attending to access issues include:

- Cataloging and classification
- Binding
- Shelving
- Circulation

Cataloging and Classification

The librarian has to decide how to catalog the instructional materials he/she has acquired. He/she has to determine what the item is about, who the possible users will be, and how to provide ready access to the item without frustrating patrons. Cataloging is the process of describing an item in a collection and classification is the logical system for arrangement of knowledge. The librarian has to decide on choice of access points. The rationale for multiple access points philosophy is that the patron is offered a variety of approaches to the item that contain the information the he/she needs. The librarian is to be mindful of the guiding principle "the reader as a focus" which emphasizes that the user is the focus in all cataloging principles and practices.[12] The choice of terms to be used as subject headings in the bibliographic records should match the terms under which patrons are most likely to search for materials. The librarian should deal with choices of synonyms, homographs, variant spellings, level of specificity of subject headings, and obsolete and current terms based on his/her knowledge of his/her patrons and of their search habits. The librarian should make good professional use of the 500 field–the general note field, to include information he/she thinks will provide more access to the materials and help patrons make informed decisions in selecting an item for possible use. The online catalog should be designed in such a way that the 500 fields are searchable. The librarian has to also decide if to catalog all the pieces or parts of an item as different items, or as a single item and/or let the physical description field, the 300 field, of the bibliographic record reflect all the part of the item as accompanying items.

Binding

Binding decisions are of importance for the instructional materials librarian. Because instructional materials are heavily used, durability of the materials is important. Teacher educators often require that students actually use these materials for assignments such as curriculum design, lesson plans, and instructional activities. Sometimes in spite of all precautions, materials still have to be bound to ensure durability. Furthermore, the nature of a good number of the instructional materials is quite unique because they come in different shapes, sizes, formats, and physical presentations. For example, a kit may have multiple parts that are not easy to put on the shelf and circulate as they were bought from the publishers or the distributors. Often the librarian has to make some resourceful binding and packaging decisions. Some puzzles, blocks, games, simulations have numerous parts and the librarian has to decide how to package them to avoid missing, or mixing up some of the parts with other items. It is not impossible to find pieces that do not belong in a bag, case, or folders. The librarian has to decide how to best bind and package the multiple parts of an instructional item to facilitate storage, shelving, retrieval, access, and use. There are some supplies that the librarian has to purchase to ease these problems. These include: bags and boxes in various sizes, special shelves, hanging rods, and map and poster cases.

Shelving

At all times the librarian has to be mindful of the fact that patrons will use only materials they can locate either online or through browsing. The aesthetic display or shelving of the materials will enhance their access and promote their use by patrons. Concern for the preservation or safety of the instructional materials must not inhibit access. If materials are put in containers such as bags and boxes, they should be displayed in such a way that patrons can see them and get attracted to use them. In spite of the irregular shapes and sizes of the materials, the instructional materials center should be kept attractive, tidy, orderly, and clean.

Security of Materials

Due to the nature of the instructional materials deciding where to place sensitizers and barcodes could be challenging decisions. The librarian has to decide if he/she is to barcode each part and/or piece of an item or to place just one barcode on the main container in which the multiple parts are placed. Most librarians have found that when video cassettes are desensitized for circulation, the information on them are either destroyed or rendered defective. The librarian has to resolve this problem. Some libraries decide not to desensitize their video cassettes as a means of protecting them. They get library employees at the exit gate to hand the video cassettes over to the students once they have passed the sensitized gate. This issue is worth all the attention the librarian has to give to it because educational videos are expensive and budgets continue to grow increasingly leaner.

Circulation

Circulation of instructional materials could be difficult. Patrons love to be able to check out materials for use at their convenience. The librarian has to decide what to circulate and what not to circulate. Then the next issue becomes deciding the circulation policies and procedures to guide the instructional materials to be circulated. Librarians are often anxious over the fact that patrons may not be careful with the materials and return them with all the multiple parts and pieces complete and in good condition. Another circulation fear is where should instructional materials be checked out, at the main lending desk or at the instructional materials area? There exists the uneasiness that non-instructional materials staff may just be too busy to pay adequate attention to verify that all materials are complete and in good condition both when they are being checked out and checked in. When necessary include information that will facilitate proper handling of instructional materials for both library staff and patrons. For instance the librarian should put in every container a card that reads:

This kit MUST be returned in the original container and in the same condition in which it was checked out. Please return to Instructional Materials Center, Education Library, 302 John Dewey Library.

One of the strategies to easy checking for complete unit by staff and patrons is to indicate the total number of pieces or parts on the container. For example on the container paste the sign: "Check For 28 Parts." This information would enable staff and patron to count and counter count before check-out and check-in.

There will naturally be some materials that will not circulate and will be restricted to only room use. Others will circulate with special permission and for special loan period. The collection development manual should include policies and procedures to serve as guidelines for such circulation concerns.

Duplicates

Providing equity and adequate access to materials may dictate when to acquire multiple copies of an item. Some items are more heavily used than others. But when students have to wait in queue to use an item, or several students place the same item on the hold or recall lists, the librarian should consider acquiring multiple copies of such items. Items such as test preparation titles should be considered for duplication. Teacher education students prefer to be able to check out test preparation materials than to be restricted to use them only within the room. After multiple copies are acquired, the librarian has to decide where to place them. The decision to place a copy or copies on reserve, ready reference, stacks or service desk would depend on the librarian's knowledge of his/her patrons and of the best location for the item given its special features. Different loan periods may be set for these materials to enhance both access and equity. As much as possible all students should have equal access to "hot" titles.

SERVICES

Instruction

Instruction on how to access and use the materials is a valuable service to patrons. An automated public catalog system is supposed to provide easy and fast access to materials owned by the library. Patrons have to be information literate if they are to take full advantage of the benefits of an automated information system.

Interlibrary Loan

Though the decision to include instructional materials in reciprocal borrowing agreement with other libraries is not an easy decision, the librarian has to deal with it. The collection development manual should include policies and procedures to deal with interlibrary loan. When patrons repeatedly request for an item through the interlibrary loan service, the librarian should consider acquiring that item.

Hours

As much as possible the needs of patrons should drive the official hours the library is opened. Special attention should be given to the needs of non-traditional and distance education patrons. Evening and weekend hours should be considered to enhance access and equity.

Equipment

The rule of thumb should be that the instructional materials center will provide the equipment needed to access the information found in its collections irrespective of the format in which the information is stored. Currently, most instruction materials collections require the purchase of a computer to access the online catalog, databases and web pages, CD-ROM drive for the compact discs, video player for the video cassettes, tape player for the audio tapes, and DVD (Digital Video Disc or Digital Versatile Disc) player for the DVDs. It would be pertinent to include here that earphones will be needed for patrons to use as they listen to information on video and audio cassettes so that distraction and disturbance are minimized. Camcorders should be acquired by the instructional materials librarian. Students may like to record their own micro teaching or/and their own in-class activities with the goal of self observation, self-evaluation, and self-improvement. Teacher educators may also want to record students teaching activities for clinical supervision purposes. They would appreciate the opportunity to check out camcorders from the instructional materials center for these professional uses.

Space

The issue of providing space for patrons to use the instructional materials is important. Given the crucial role these materials play in teacher education, faculty and teacher education majors need adequate space to examine, review, and use these materials either individually or as a group. The faculty may like to pull out certain instructional materials and conduct a class session using them. Students may like to pull some materials to use for assignment completion or for lesson planning exercises. There are instances when students request space to rehearse integrating some of the instructional materials into lessons they are planning to teach. Sometimes they want friends and course mates to watch and critique their presentation. Therefore providing space for patrons to use the instructional materials is necessary.

BUDGET

These are days of budgetary cut and of accountability. There are numerous instructional materials available for purchase. Unfortunately, the librarian cannot buy all the items he/she would like to acquire because of the size of the budget. There are some strategies that would enable the librarian to build a relatively strong collection in spite of limited funds. They include focusing on:

- Priority areas of the teacher education programs in the parent institution
- One subject area of the collection each year
- One type of collection each year

Being aware of changes in the teacher education program or program offerings would enhance the judicious use of the budget that seems to get leaner and leaner each year.

COLLECTION MANAGEMENT AND MAINTENANCE

Collection management and maintenance activities would include repairs, replacements, collection assessment and weeding. As long as materials are in open stacks, are used, and are circulated, the librarian should expect that from time to time he/she will have to deal with damaged, mutilated, and lost items. The conspectus approach to collection analysis, though not without critics, should be used to assess the collection. Brittled, dilapidated, obsolete, ugly, broken, and incomplete materials should be repaired, replaced or weeded from the collections. There should be guidelines for these activities in the collection development manual. The policies and procedures should be realistic, feasible, and not too complex and time consuming.

CONCLUSION

"Across the country, parents and taxpayers have sent a clear message to policymakers: Improve schools to make sure our children have the knowledge and skills they need to succeed. Spend more if necessary, taxpayers say, but require schools to produce results."[13] The instructional materials collections have three main goals. They are to:

1. Support the teacher education programs especially the methods and practicum courses in the teacher education programs and sometimes includes the children's, juvenile and young adult literature courses in the school of education.
2. Collect and make available quality materials for inspection, evaluation, and use.
3. Provide educational resources that focus on the teaching profession, staff and personal development of veteran, novice, and prospective teachers.

When educators and education librarians talk about collection or collections they may be talking about a concept that may not make sense to people who are not in education. Given the purposes and uses of instructional materials, collection development may be viewed from a whole different perspective. This article has attempted to identify some instructional materials that could seem strange to those not directly involved with the education of children or with the preparation of professionals charged with the responsibility of teaching in such a way that all children, irrespective of their diversity or exceptionalities, learn curricular contents. The librarian charged with developing and maintaining instructional materials collections has a challenging but interesting task.

REFERENCES

1. Gall, Meredith D. 1981. *Handbook for Evaluating and Selecting Curriculum Materials*. Boston: Alyn and Bacon, Inc. p. 5.

2. NCATE. 2001. "What to Look for in a Teacher Preparation Program" http://www.ncate.org/future/lookfor.htm (Accessed on October 21, 2002.) p. 1.

3. Wise, Arthur E. 2001. "NCATE: Performance-Based Accreditation: Reform in Action." http://www.ncate.org/newsbrfs/reforminaction.htm. [2002, October 21] p.1.

4. MacEwan, Bonnie. "Understanding Users' Needs and Making Collections Choices." *Library Collections, Acquisitions, & Technical Services*, 23, no. 3 (1999): p. 315.

5. Ryan, Kevin and Cooper, James M. 1998. *Kaleidoscope: Readings in Education,* 8th Edition. Boston: Houghton Mifflin Co. p. 495.

6. "What are Simulations and Games." http://216.239.51.100/search?q=cache: OPo6FJA6edIC:www.education.uts.edu.au/ozsaga/about.HTML+Simulations+and+Games& hl=en&ie=UTF-8. [2002, November 12] p. 1.

7. Intner, Sheila S. and Weihs, Jean. 1990. *Standard Cataloging for School and Public Libraries*. Littleton, Colo.: Libraries Unlimited. p. 22.

8. "How Teaching Matters" in "ETS Study Validates Premise Underlying NCATE Standards Affirms More than Subject Matter Knowledge Necessary for Effective Teaching." http://www.ncate.org/newsbrfs/etshowteachmatters.htm [2002, November 8] p. 1.

9. "Fruits and Vegetable." http://www.geocities.com/Heartland/Acres/7875/fruits.html [2002, November 13] p. 2.

10. "Allouette" http://www3.sympatico.ca/cottagecountry/songs/a-alou.htm [2002, November 13].

11. "About AskERIC" http://askeric.org/About/ [2002, November 11] p. 1.

12. Chan, Lois Mai. 1986. *Library of Congress Subject Headings: Principles and Application*. 2nd Edition. Littleton, Colo.: Libraries Unlimited. p. 18.

13. Educational Testing Services. "Let's Talk about Testing." http://www.ets.org/testing/index.html [2002, November 12] p. 1.

Cooperation Between Collection Development and Cataloging: A Policy for Proposing Projects to Cataloging Services

Rebecca L. Mugridge

SUMMARY. This paper discusses how three developments in the Pennsylvania State University Libraries Cataloging Services department allowed it to clear out most of its cataloging backlog. These three developments were (1) the reorganization of the department into format-based, self-directed work teams, (2) training staff to create original cataloging and authority control records, and (3) the implementation of PromptCat. These developments allowed Cataloging Services to accept a number of project proposals from selectors. Cataloging Services worked with Collection Development librarians to develop policies and procedures for proposing projects to cataloging, and to set priorities for those projects based on library goals and initiatives. *[Article copies available for a fee from The Haworth Document Delivery Service: 1-800-HAWORTH. E-mail address: <docdelivery@haworthpress.com> Website: <http://www.HaworthPress.com> © 2003 by The Haworth Press, Inc. All rights reserved.]*

KEYWORDS. Cataloging, collection development, policies, cooperative projects, technical services

---

Rebecca L. Mugridge is Head of Cataloging Services, The Pennsylvania State University Libraries, 126 Paterno Library, University Park, PA 16802 (E-mail: rlm31@psu.edu).

[Haworth co-indexing entry note]: "Cooperation Between Collection Development and Cataloging: A Policy for Proposing Projects to Cataloging Services." Mugridge, Rebecca L. Co-published simultaneously in *The Acquisitions Librarian* (The Haworth Information Press, an imprint of The Haworth Press, Inc.) No. 30, 2003, pp. 155-163; and: *Collection Development Policies: New Directions for Changing Collections* (ed: Daniel C. Mack) The Haworth Information Press, an imprint of The Haworth Press, Inc., 2003, pp. 155-163. Single or multiple copies of this article are available for a fee from The Haworth Document Delivery Service [1-800-HAWORTH, 9:00 a.m. - 5:00 p.m. (EST). E-mail address: docdelivery@haworthpress.com].

http://www.haworthpress.com/store/product.asp?sku=J101
© 2003 by The Haworth Press, Inc. All rights reserved.
10.1300/J101v15n30_12

INTRODUCTION

Many large research libraries' cataloging departments struggle constantly with a cataloging backlog. Because of the emphasis on cataloging currently-received materials, presumably of greater interest in current research, those cataloging departments often find it difficult to find the time and resources to participate in special cataloging projects. Often, retrospective conversion projects do not happen unless outside funding is identified and earmarked for the project, and special staff are often hired to pursue those projects. Similarly, recataloging or reclassification projects are difficult to find time for, as it's difficult to justify spending time on materials that have at least some access in the online catalog when there are other materials that have no access whatsoever, or when there are current receipts waiting to be processed.

Penn State University Libraries has managed, through three major changes in Cataloging Services, to effectively eliminate the backlog of current receipts. This has allowed the department to pursue many projects that have been requested by customer libraries. An understanding of Cataloging Services' organizational structure, its reorganization in 1995, and other changes implemented since that time will help show how this has happened.

BACKGROUND

In 1995, the Pennsylvania State University Libraries' Cataloging Services was formed into six self-directed work teams. The formation of the self-directed work teams followed closely on the heels of the acquisitions department's formation into teams in 1994. After the reorganization Cataloging Services consisted of five format-based cataloging teams and the CatMarking Team (responsible for labelling, security stripping, stamping, and barcoding library materials). The five format-based teams addressed monographs (print, electronic and microform), music and AV materials, cartographic materials, rare books, and serials.[1] Cataloging Services does all of the cataloging for 22 of Penn State's 24 campuses, as well as transfers, withdrawals, recataloging and general maintenance.

After the reorganization,[2] the department was managed by three Cataloging Coordinators, two of whom were librarians, the third a high-level staff member. After the retirement of one of the librarian Cataloging Coordinators, the department was managed through 1999 by the two remaining coordinators. They divided the duties of managing the department between them, with one taking responsibility for managing the work of the librarians in the department and the other managing the staff.[3] The librarians in the department were each assigned to particular cataloging teams as resource persons, based on their area of expertise, an organizational structure that continues to this day. They do not have supervisory responsibility over the staff on the teams; rather, they are responsible for original cataloging and helping staff with difficult cataloging questions, and they share responsibility with others on their respective teams for training, documentation, and liaison with customers.[4]

One of the greatest advantages of forming into format-based teams was that by assigning teams to handle particular types of material, it was possible to give some of our customers attention that had never been possible before. For example, before the existence of the Special Collections Cataloging Team, material acquired by the three special collections areas at Penn State (University Archives, Historical Collections and Labor Archives, and the Rare Book Room), received little attention from Cataloging. The emphasis in cataloging was to get the new material out, presumably because that would be of greatest interest to most researchers. After forming the format-based teams, each of our customers had cataloging staff assigned to catalog and process their material, so their collections quickly became more accessible through representation in our online catalog.

Like other universities where the librarians have faculty status, it was and is difficult for the librarians to find time to do significant amounts of original cataloging. Although the amount of material requiring original cataloging is small (currently around 3,000 titles per year), by the mid-1990s it had accumulated into significant backlogs in each faculty member's area of expertise. This was addressed at Penn State by teaching staff members how to do original cataloging as well as how to create authority records through the Library of Congress Program for Cooperative Cataloging Name Authority Cooperative program (NACO). This started off as a small effort, but has grown so that at this point in time, there are nine staff members in Cataloging Services who do some amount of original cataloging. Because original cataloging had formerly only been performed by professional librarians, it was considered to be professional-level work. Therefore, these positions went through a job audit, and they were all upgraded according to the percentage that each position's responsibilities were devoted to original cataloging work as opposed to complex copy cataloging (non-book formats, foreign-language material, etc.) or basic copy cataloging (English-language material, book format).

The end result of training staff to perform original cataloging is that, with one exception,[5] there is now no backlog of original cataloging in the department. In general, because of the smaller number of items needing original cataloging and the large number of staff and faculty who perform original cataloging, new receipts that need original cataloging will often take less time to get to the shelf than those that require copy cataloging. The Monographs Team, for example, has set a goal to get materials requiring original cataloging to the shelf within two weeks, although it usually takes less time than that. Additionally, items that are needed quickly can be cataloged within four hours or three days (our two categories of rush processing), depending on the urgency required.

Also in the mid-1990s, Technical Services implemented two other changes in its processing that improved its efficiencies. The first change involved PromptCat Services. We began to receive cataloging records from OCLC's PromptCat Service for all items that we received through our Yankee Book Peddler approval plan. This currently represents 22% of our processing. The second change was training acquisitions staff to perform cataloging upon receipt. Although these two changes were accompanied by the loss of several staff positions, overall there was a net gain in efficiency by taking some of the processing out of Cataloging Services, allowing the department to turn its attention to other needs.

The final result of these three developments: training staff to do original cataloging, implementing PromptCat Services, and allowing acquisitions staff to do cataloging upon receipt for some materials, is that by the fall of 2000, Cataloging Services had very little backlogged materials. Because of this, Cataloging Services has been able to accept a number of project proposals from the various customer libraries around the University. One more development should probably be explained before going any further. In 1999 The University Libraries reorganized into a subject library system. At University Park, in one building there now exists multiple subject libraries which each have their own reference desk and reference collection. They are each managed by a head librarian, and have their own staff and librarians.[6] Cataloging Services considers each of these libraries to be a customer, and many of the libraries have projects, large and small, that they would like to have addressed by Cataloging Services.

PROJECTS PROPOSED TO CATALOGING SERVICES

Project proposals range in size from the very small to the very extensive and fall into four main categories:

- Reclassification
- Retrospective conversion
- Creating analytic records for materials formerly cataloged as a set
- Cataloging small pockets of materials that might be otherwise overlooked.

Some examples of projects that are currently being worked on by Cataloging Services teams are:

Monographs Team

- Retrospective conversion and reclassification of Pennsylvania state documents
- Retrospective conversion and reclassification of Pennsylvania local documents
- Transfer of 325 high-use classics materials from the Libraries' off-site annex to the main library
- Recatalog approximately 180 volumes in the *Topics in current chemistry series* for the Physical Sciences Library (currently cataloged as a set, requested to be cataloged separately but classed together)

Maps Cataloging Team

- Retrospective conversion of approximately 33,000 maps for the Maps Library
- Cataloging of 423 Pennsylvania maps needing mostly original cataloging

Special Collections Cataloging Team

- Cataloging of 8th Air Force Collection for the Historical Collections and Labor Archives (a unit of the Special Collections Library)
- Cataloging of the Chris Gaines Memorial Collection, approximately 5,000 items on the Amish

Music/AV Cataloging Team

- Catalog approximately 600 scores from the Alice Marshall Collection of women's history and literature housed at the Penn State Harrisburg Campus Library
- Catalog a gift collection of approximately 2,000 jazz sound recordings

Each of Cataloging Services' cataloging teams has a projects page with a variety of projects either being considered or worked on at any given time.[7] While each team has created team web pages that reflect its own personality, each of the projects pages are consistent in that they list:

- The name of the project
- A brief description of the project
- Contact names of persons responsible in both the cataloging team and the requesting library
- Expected start and completion dates
- Current project status

NEED FOR A POLICY STATEMENT

In the spring of 2001, it became obvious that not all selectors were aware that they could propose projects to Cataloging Services, or to whom to make a proposal. Part of the confusion may have arisen from the reorganization into teams, although that had happened years earlier. One of the results of that reorganization was that the teams were managing their own workflow and setting many of their own priorities. While those priorities were in accordance with departmental guidelines, each decision was not necessarily run past the cataloging coordinators or department head. Another possible cause for confusion was that librarians who came to Penn State from other institutions very often had no experience with team management and organization. Often these librarians found it difficult to get used to the idea of working outside of the hierarchical structure and felt more comfortable addressing queries directly to the department head. In order to address this confusion, the Assistant Dean for Collections appointed a small group to look at how projects were proposed, accepted and prioritized, make recommendations for changes if needed, and document the process for inclusion in the Libraries selectors manual. The group included four librarians, including the author.

When the group met, it quickly became clear that selectors were not dissatisfied with how things were currently working. Rather, there was simply a need to document the process and share the policy with all librarians. Up to this point, project requests would be sent to either the team, a team leader, the cataloging coordinator or the department head. Whomever it was sent to, it would be forwarded as needed, to get to the right person or persons who needed to be involved. That process would be basically invisible to the requestor. A contact person on the appropriate team would be assigned, and that person would be responsible for apprising the requesting librarian of the planned starting date, estimated finishing date, and progress of the project. Once procedures were written, reviewed and approved, the project would begin on an agreed-upon date.

Although for the most part the current process was working well, one area that Cataloging Services was interested in clarifying was the setting of priorities. Sometimes it's very clear that a project is high priority. For example, a cataloging project being funded by a National Endowment for Humanities grant has to be completed by a certain date defined by the grant; therefore, it immediately becomes high priority.

The issue of project priority is greatest for the Monographs Team because they catalog for all subject and campus libraries and their time is the most in demand. The other cataloging teams have a more narrow customer base, so the competition for time and attention is less severe. For example, while the Maps Cataloging Team will catalog cartographic materials for any of the subject or campus libraries, their primary customers are the Maps Library, the Earth and Mineral Sciences Library, and the Special Collections Library. Whereas the Maps Cataloging Team currently has seven project proposals listed on its projects web page, the Monographs Team has well over 30 project proposals from six libraries to consider. Therefore, it is clear that setting priorities is a critical issue for Cataloging Services in general, and the Monographs Team in particular.

For the great majority of library projects, however, it is not clear what priority should be assigned. Cataloging Services did not want to be in a position of assigning priorities to the various projects proposed by all of the various libraries at Penn State. Similarly, allowing the librarian proposing the project to assign the priority also did not seem appropriate. For most librarians, their own material is critical for research, timely, etc., and the temptation might exist for them to always assign a high priority to their own projects. As a compromise, the group's recommendation was to set a low priority to all projects unless the project was (1) first discussed by the Collection Development Group Leaders and (2) they agreed on an alternate priority assignment. The Collection Development Group Leaders is a committee that is made up of representatives from all of the University Park subject and branch libraries, as well as two librarians representing the campus libraries. These librarians work together to make collection development decisions affecting all of the libraries, and seemed to be the appropriate body to weigh in on this issue.

The complete recommendation of the group follows:

The current procedure for proposing projects to Cataloging is working well. The procedure is to contact the team involved (using the team's global email address), proposing the project. The Head of Cataloging and Assistant to the Head of Cataloging should always be copied on that initial email, so that they can make sure that the team discusses the project, assigns a project contact person, writes procedures/guidelines if necessary, and in general monitor the progress of the project.

Selectors and collection development librarians should make recommendations concerning project priorities, and Cataloging will accommodate them as much as possible. All proposed projects will be automatically assigned a low priority,[8] unless the Collection Development Group Leaders decide otherwise.

To summarize, the overall process would be:

1. Selector proposes project to Team, copying the Head of Cataloging and Assistant to the Head of Cataloging on the email.
2. If the project proposal is anything other than low priority, the selector brings it to CDGL for discussion first (taking into account other projects the Team is already working on).
3. Selector communicates the priority decision to the Team involved.
4. Team, including the faculty resource person (along with the Head of Cataloging and Assistant to the Head of Cataloging, if necessary) works with the selector to implement the project.

This recommendation was shared with both Cataloging Services and all selectors and approved without changes.

CONCLUSION

It has been very useful for Cataloging Services to examine the processes by which subject and campus libraries propose projects for consideration. By asking those responsible for the Libraries collection development policies, procedures and decisions to have a role in the setting of project priorities, we have put more of the decision-making power into the hands of those who are best able to evaluate those decisions.

ENDNOTES

1. The Serials Cataloging Team has since become part of the Serials Department, formed in 2000.

2. For more information on the reorganization of Penn State University Libraries Cataloging Services, see Marie L. Bednar, Roger Brisson, and Judy Hewes' "Pursuing the Three Ts: How Total Quality Management, Technology, and Teams Transformed the Cataloging Department at Penn State," *Cataloging & Classification Quarterly* 30. no 2/3 (2000) 241-79. The current organizational chart can be found at: http://www.libraries.psu.edu/iasweb/catsweb/org/org.htm.

3. This has since been changed by hiring a Department Head to take the place of one of the Cataloging Coordinators, who retired in 1999.

4. For more about the role of the Cataloging Faculty in Penn State University Libraries Cataloging Services department see Rosann Bazirjian, "Role of Library Faculty in a Team Environment," *Library Administration and Management* 17.1 (2003.Winter) 33-39.

5. The Special Collections Cataloging Team is a fairly new unit in the department. It was originally called the Rare Book Team, and primarily cataloged monographic material for the Rare Books Room and the two archival units. It has only been since 2000 that the team has begun to do all cataloging for the three units, which were at that time formed into one library: The Special Collections Library. The Manuscripts Cataloging Librarian became part of Cataloging Services in 2001, and has in 2002 begun to teach one staff member to catalog manuscript material, hopefully with more staff to follow.

6. See http://www.libraries.psu.edu/libs.html for the full listing of Penn State's subject and campus libraries.

7. See http://www.libraries.psu.edu/iasweb/catsweb/dept/projfrm.htm for a listing of each Team's projects.

8. A low priority does not mean that a project will not be addressed quickly; rather, it means that it does not have a "drop everything" status. Often Cataloging Services works simultaneously on projects with high and low priority. This depends on the subject and language expertise of the department. For example, if a high priority project requires the cataloger to be fluent in Russian, the Slavic-language cataloger will give it a high priority, while the other catalogers in the department are free to work on other projects.

Index

Numbers followed by *n* indicate a note; those followed by *nn* indicate notes.

http://www.haworthpress.com/store/product.asp?sku=J101
© 2003 by The Haworth Press, Inc. All rights reserved.

SPECIAL 25%-OFF DISCOUNT!

Order a copy of this book with this form or online at:
http://www.haworthpress.com/store/product.asp?sku=5067
Use Sale Code BOF25 in the online bookshop to receive 25% off!

Collection Development Policies
New Directions for Changing Collections

____ in softbound at $18.71 (regularly $24.95) (ISBN: 0-7890-1471-8)
____ in hardbound at $29.96 (regularly $39.95) (ISBN: 0-7890-1470-X)

COST OF BOOKS _____

Outside USA/ Canada/
Mexico: Add 20% _____

POSTAGE & HANDLING _____
(US: $4.00 for first book & $1.50
for each additional book)
Outside US: $5.00 for first book
& $2.00 for each additional book)

SUBTOTAL _____

in Canada: add 7% GST _____

STATE TAX _____
(NY, OH, & MIN residents please
add appropriate local sales tax

FINAL TOTAL _____
(if paying in Canadian funds, convert
using the current exchange rate,
UNESCO coupons welcome)

❑ **BILL ME LATER:** ($5 service charge will be added)
(Bill-me option is good on US/Canada/
Mexico orders only; not good to jobbers,
wholesalers, or subscription agencies.)

❑ **Signature** _____

❑ **Payment Enclosed: $** _____

❑ **PLEASE CHARGE TO MY CREDIT CARD:**

❑ Visa ❑ MasterCard ❑ AmEx ❑ Discover
❑ Diner's Club ❑ Eurocard ❑ JCB

Account #_____

Exp Date _____

Signature_____
*(Prices in US dollars and subject to
change without notice.)*

PLEASE PRINT ALL INFORMATION OR ATTACH YOUR BUSINESS CARD

Name		
Address		
City	State/Province	Zip/Postal Code
Country		
Tel	Fax	
E-Mail		

May we use your e-mail address for confirmations and other types of information? ❑Yes❑ No
We appreciate receiving your e-mail address. Haworth would like to e-mail special discount
offers to you, as a preferred customer. **We will never share, rent, or exchange your e-mail
address.** We regard such actions as an invasion of your privacy.

Order From Your Local Bookstore or Directly From
The Haworth Press, Inc.
10 Alice Street, Binghamton, New York 13904-1580 • USA
Call Our toll-free number (1-800-429-6784) / Outside US/Canada: (607) 722-5857
Fax: 1-800-895-0582 / Outside US/Canada: (607) 771-0012
E-Mail your order to us: Orders@haworthpress.com

Please Photocopy this form for your personal use.
www.HaworthPress.com   BOF03